Turning Points
in
Religious Life

Turning Points
in
Religious Life

Edited by

Carol Quigley, I.H.M.

Michael Glazier
Wilmington, Delaware

First published in 1987 by Michael Glazier, Inc. 1935 West Fourth Street, Wilmington Delaware 19805. ©1987 by Carol Quigley, I.H.M. All rights reserved. Library of Congress Catalog Card Number: 85-45565.
International Standard Book Number: 0-89453-545-5.
Cover design by Lillian Brulc.
Printed in the United States of America.

Table of Contents

Section Two
Congregational Leaders Speak

Preface

The year was 1965. The setting, the Second Vatican Council. The document, *Perfectae Caritatis*, an invitation to religious congregations to renew themselves, to look to their roots, to experiment. In Monroe, Michigan, the Sisters, Servants of the Immaculate Heart of Mary, were ready to do just that. We were 120 years old, enjoying a satisfying period of young life, acclaimed leadership in the burgeoning field of Catholic education. In peak years of such promise why should the IHMs look at all? Why were we ready, even eager, to examine ourselves, renew ourselves? For us, times seemed indeed good.

But were times that good? It took the world-view leaders of Vatican II to point up that times had changed, had in fact, been hurrying along for many years, that a veritable chasm yawned between the world of the 1870's Vatican I and the "global village" world of Vatican II. In Rome the Spirit descended on the assembled church leaders; its tongues of fire spread over the entire world, swept away a static church, ushered in the dynamic church of New Testament times.

All across the country, congregations of women religious began to draw up models of structure change designed to meet the needs and demands of this new era of Church History. Among the Monroe IHMs the small stirrings of pre-Vatican II days erupted into a groundswell. Teachers for more than a century, we stopped short, took a hard look at ourselves, re-defined our call to ministry, wrote new lesson plans, envisioned the church not so much in the image of a pearl, but a seed to be planted deep in the earth whenever and wherever our ministry called us. Through more than a decade we pushed forward, sometimes with grace, sometimes not so gracefully, until we arrived at the Congregational Chapter, 1982.

By then as a congregation we had come to know that even as we cherished our past, held fast to the changeless amidst the changing, there could be no turning back to pre-Vatican II times. We had spent nearly a generation of personal renewal in prayer integrated with the gospel-call to justice and peace. The time had come to push forward not only as individuals but together, as a corporate body, the IHM Monroe Community.

"Effective renewal and right adaptation cannot be achieved save with the cooperation of all the members." That statement from *Perfectae Caritatis* and our own experience for the past years prompted the chapter delegates of 1982 to request the governing board to coordinate a continuing process of Corporate Renewal as a complement to the personal renewal we had entered into during the 1960s and 1970s. Members of the governing board drew up a five-year plan, its overall aim an invitation to conversion of heart and life, to the "refounding" of the congregation, and to the empowerment of ourselves and others to Christian life. We chose TURNING POINTS as the central image, the focal point of our efforts to "re-found" the congregation in its pristine values of gospel risk and discipleship.

During the first years of our Corporate Renewal, 1983, in small groups we shared with each other the personal turning points of our own lives. In 1984 we studied the History of Religious life, remembered together the turning points during the long years from earliest New Testament times to the present. During 1985, our 140th anniversary, we reflected on our corporate turning points as IHMs through retreats on our constitutions. In 1986 we traced the turning points of our congregation in mission. 1987 will be a jubilee-celebration year of the turning points of all our lives.

The articles in this book are the result of our 1984 year of Corporate Renewal; the study of: The History of Religious Life, The Theology of the Vows, Authority in the Church, Canonical Status. We are pleased to share with our readers some of the richness we experienced when we examined religious life and its multiple turning points over so many years. The four themes were originally presented as talks in community gatherings. Each contributor accepts responsibility for her/his statements. The second section of the volume is authored by leadership. To commemorate Founder's Day, November 10, 1984, and to symbolize our own corporateness, the four living general superiors, leaders during a thirty-year period, presented to more than 700 Sisters in Monroe their reflections on the final theme for the year: Religious Life and Its Future. The gathering of Sisters on that particular date, we know, represented only one small segment of the many Catholic Sisterhoods involved in the quest for growth and spiritual becoming.

In presenting this book, I wish to express my appreciation to the committee members who planned and coordinated the Corporate Renewal Series: Sisters Juliana Casey, Mary Jo Maher, Alice Miller. Likewise I am grateful to Sisters Prudentia Brand, Ellen Clanon, Annunciata Grix, Margaret Ann Henige for their special assistance. In particular, the congregation honors the memory of one contributor, Emily George, RSM, whose life ended tragically in a car accident on December 6, 1984.

To all Sisters, Servants of the Immaculate Heart of Mary, whose presence confirmed our call to Corporate Renewal, and whose daily lives give witness to the words written here, we dedicate this volume.

Carol Quigley, I.H.M.

Monroe, Michigan
November 10, 1986

Section One
Turning Points
in the
History of Religious Life

Reflections on the History of Religious Life and Contemporary Development

Sandra Marie Schneiders, IHM

Lecture I:
Overview of the History of Religious Life

I. INTRODUCTION

The subject I have been asked to address in the very brief space of three lectures, is the history of religious life: 2000 years of Christian experience and the implications of that experience for contemporary religious! For psychological as well as logical reasons I will begin with the heavier material. This first lecture will deal with what we might call the historical data, some of the facts which history yields about the experience of religious life in the Church. On the basis of that data we will then reflect, in Lectures II and III, on some of the implications, patterns, challenges, and suggestions which that history addresses to us.

A. Purposes of the Historical Section of the Corporate Renewal Lectures

As we assemble information about our collective past—and the past of religious life as such—we must approach it the same way we approach the study of the history of any institution or group. First we hope, by studying our history, to avoid errors that have already been made and which we do not want to repeat.

Secondly, historical awareness enables us to escape imprisonment in the present and determinism about the future. Many experiences of the past twenty or twenty-five years have helped to jar us out of the frozen mindset of the post-Tridentine period. However, we can be imprisoned not only in the past but also in the present if we are not aware that our own time is just as much an historical period as any in the past. Our form of religious life is as relative, time-conditioned, and passing as were the forms of earlier times. We can also be victims of the future, imprisoned in determinism, in the resigned conviction that there is no way of avoiding a predetermined fate, that what is coming is coming and we have no control over it. A study of history can liberate us from both imprisonment in the present and determinism about the future.

Thirdly, we look to history in order to find ways to utilize the resources of our corporate past for our present tasks, for rethinking and recreating our life in the present. We hope to develop a healthy, constructive, creative, imaginative attitude toward the role of time in our individual and corporate lives. History is one of those disciplines which has been rethought in foundational ways since the 1800s. We are probably the first generation in history to *know* that we are historical agents, to realize that history is not simply events which took place in the past but that history is constitutive of our being. We are historical beings and history is what we do, not simply what happens to us.

B. Attitudes Toward History

Certain attitudes toward history can shape our approach to our collective past. I want to call attention to a few of these, some of which can be quite dysfunctional and others of which are more helpful.

Among the dysfunctional attitudes toward history is the persuasion that whatever came first in any historical development is necessarily the best. We use expressions like: "This is the original, or primordial, or primitive, or foundational event or formualation." These are all positive statements, and many times they are correct statements about origins. But they can create the impression that things have been going steadily downhill ever since. Plato is supposed to have remarked that the younger generation was going to the dogs. Presumably the process of decline was well underway by the 5th century B.C.! Martin Heidegger brought this notion into contemporary philosophy with his theory that the further away we get from the beginning of something the more attenuated it gets. This simply is not true. Some things do get weaker as they get further away from their origin but some things get better as they grow and develop.

A second dysfunctional attitude toward history arises from the search for the classical. We are convinced that there was some period that represented the paradigmatic perfection of the phenomenon in question. If only we could find that classical period we could model ourselves on the pattern. One sometimes hears members of a religious order say, "If we could just identify that period in our history when we were the most successful, the most united, the most developed, we could go back to that." But, of course, there is no going back.

A third dysfunctional attitude which we have recently heard defended in the Church is that history brings about only accidental changes; that historical changes are merely superficial modifications of some enduring essence. True historical thinking makes us well aware of the falsity of this position. There is no such thing as an historical phenomenon which is essentially the same in all places and at all times and which undergoes merely accidental modifications. For those of us who have been intellectually raised in scholastic philosophy with its static Aristotelian foundations, there is a tendency to think in these terms without realizing it, and so to keep asking for the essence of things, the unchanging substances of changing phenomena.

A fourth dysfunctional attitude is perhaps the opposite of

the essentialist attitude, namely, a rather thorough-going relativism which maintains that nothing is of any more value than anything else. Such an attitude maintains that every age had its particular characteristics, beliefs, attitudes and, that as one goes through history, one discovers that such characteristics were as good for their own age as ours are for our time. Whatever future ages produce, it will be neither better nor worse than what our time has produced. In other words, no value judgment can be made on anything because everything everywhere is always changing. It is true that everything is changing; but it is not true that we cannot make value judgments about developments.

A final dysfunctional attitude is the tendency to think that history refers only to the past, whereas the present is a kind of a-historical reality. History is the way human beings are constituted. We are essentially time-constructed creatures, that is, we are the place of the simultaneous interaction of past, present and future. There is no past except in us. There is no future except in us. The present is the place where past and future interact to constitute us as essentially historical beings. In other words, history is our present as well as our past, and our past is a fund of possibility out of which we must construct the present in the light of the future.

Let us now look at some healthy attitudes which are partly the product of the revision of history which has gone on since the late 19th century. This revision has led first of all to the realization that history is not a collection of events strung like beads on a string. Rather, it is a process in which we are all involved, not simply as entities carried along in a kind of stream that exists outside of us, but as agents who are literally doing history, making history, being history. This realization can engender in us a creative and responsible attitude toward our role in history.

A second healthy attitude engendered by a modern understanding of history is an appropriate relativizion of our experience. The more we know about history, the more convinced we become that things we might have thought of as set in concrete, at some time did not exist. This need not lead to relativism; it should rather lead to a healthy relativity. In other words, it does not lead to the conclusion that everything is equal, but it does lead to the conclusion that nothing created is absolute. We can make value judgments. We can say that some periods in history were more vital than others. But we must also realize that no period of history with regard to any phenomenon, including religious life, is absolute.

A third benefit of a modern historical consciousness is the liberation of the imagination from its imprisonment in the *status quo*. If we cannot imagine things differently, we cannot work for change. As many of us know from personal experience in counseling or spiritual direction, if a person cannot imagine her or his life differently, she or he cannot make any progress toward a changed and improved life. The imagination is the faculty of development and growth. As we learn how different things have been in the past, we can imagine how different things can be in the future. Furthermore, things can change significantly without disintegrating. This attitude is incompatible, however, with the essentialist mentality. If one thinks of religious life as an essence, then if one removes any "essential element" the life itself necessarily collapses, for essential elements are factors which must be present for a thing to exist. An historical perspective can make us aware that almost every element of religious life as we know it has, at one historical period or another, not been part of that life.

A fourth advantage of an historical awareness is that it helps us to perceive trends and patterns which can be very illuminating for our interpretation of present experience. One of the things a counselor tries to help people do with their individual histories is to see patterns in their attitudes, behaviors, and relationships. To understand trends is to be able to recognize the beginning of an internal process which leads to bad or good results. Thus, one can learn how one makes decisions, how one gradually slips into depression or becomes violently angry. One learns to discern patterns in one's personal history, patterns which illuminate the interpretation of present experience. If we can do this for ourselves as individuals, we can also do it with our corporate existence as a religious congregation.

Finally, from the study of history we also learn that there is no such thing as "bare facts." All data, to be meaningful, must be interpreted. It would not do a person any good to know the facts of her childhood if they remained uninterpreted. If all history is interpretation, somebody is doing the interpreting. It is well for us to be aware that every interpreter has her or his agenda which may be valid or suspect. The great 19th century masters of suspicion, Marx, Nietzsche and Freud, have helped us to develop what Ricoeur refers to as a "hermeneutics of suspicion." This theory of interpretation alerts us to the possible distortion of history by interpreters who have something to gain, lose, or protect by interpreting data in a certain way. For example, if we look at the great treatises on virginity of the 3rd and 4th centuries, we read some very beautiful material; but we are also aware that these treatises contain a strong strain of Manichaean-inspired anti-sexuality that was operative in Christianity during that period. This dangerous bias is built into those treatises, not because anyone intended to pervert the understanding of Christian virginity, but because this bias was part of the interpretive framework of some Fathers of the Church.

Ricoeur, however, makes another important point about historical interpretation, namely, that we also need a "hermeneutics of retrieval" to complement the hermeneutics of suspicion. Marx, Nietzsche and Freud were basically concerned with undermining false consciousness. Although they did a very good job of exposing the deception in appearances, they sometimes had a hard time discovering the valuable and true amid the debris. Ricoeur makes the point that our interpretative process must also allow us to bring forward that which is valuable even when it is mixed with much that is false or suspect. A pure hermeneutics of suspicion would lead us to write off the entire development of consecrated virginity and celibacy in the Church as the product of disturbed minds, the sacralization of a Manichaean fear of sex. Such evaluations of virginity have been proposed. However, a hermeneutics of retrieval, while taking seriously the problematic influence of anti-sexuality in the development of consecrated celibacy, refuses to admit that that is the whole story. It searches the record for the healthy and holy content of this movement and seeks to liberate the valuable from that which must be repudiated. These two forms of interpretation must complement each other. On the one hand, the hermeneutics of suspicion keeps us from naively affirming that whatever was thought or done in the "good old days" must have been right and good, holy and inspired by purely spiritual motives. On the other hand, the hermeneutics of retrieval says that something for which holy people gave their lives must be, at root, worthwhile. The problem is to discern the true from the false, the virtuous from the sick, and to build the future of the tradition on solid ground.

II. AN OVERVIEW OF THE HISTORY OF ROMAN CATHOLIC RELIGIOUS LIFE IN THE WEST

Keeping in mind these ideas about history, let us take a look at Roman Catholic religious life in the West. Although religious life is undergoing a revival in some Protestant denominations, and is still relatively strong in the Eastern Church (there are between 500 and 600 Eastern rite religious in the United States today and a significant number of Protestant religious following the Benedictine or Franciscan rules), I will not be discussing these phenomena.

A. First and Second Centuries: Virgins and Widows

We start with a difficult question: When did religious life begin? Most histories of religious life assert that it began in the 3rd and 4th centuries with the flight of many Christians to the desert. This dating reflects what we have discovered to be true of almost all historical studies up to our own time, namely, that phenomena which originated with or were dominated by women do not get into the historical accounts.

The non-telling of women's stories, whether in politics, art, domestic life, economics, theology, or the spiritual life, is generally characteristic of mainstream historiography. History was written by men, for men, and about men. My research convinces me that the history of religious life begins in the New Testament period, i.e., before the end of the first century. There were in the Church in this early period rather large numbers of enrolled widows and consecrated virgins. Justin Martyr tells us there were a few men among the virgins. The widows were, of course, all women. The development of religious life in the first and second centuries, which I regard as absolutely foundational, was basically a feminine phenomenon. That may be why it usually does not get into the history books, or, when it does, is minimized.

Let us examine this early phenomenon. In New Testament times, in I Timothy 5:9-16 for example, we have references to widows who are described as older women who had been married once, whose spouses had died, who had properly seen to the upbringing of their minor chldren, and who were outstanding in virtue in the community. These women were enrolled in a kind of *ordo* in the Church within which they ministered to the needs of the community. They were also outstanding for their life of prayer. This group, mentioned in the New Testament, had by the 3rd century almost disappeared as an *ordo* and such women became known in the community as deacons. Sometimes they were referred to as deaconesses, but it seems more to our purpose to call them deacons because they were ordained, members of an *ordo* in the Church which lasted until about the 6th century, and whose members functioned much the way our permanent deacons do today. They belonged to the local community and served its needs. After the 6th century the *ordo* of women deacons was suppressed and the ordination of women was forbidden.

During the same period, there were other consecrated women, called virgins. While the widows were supposed to be at least 60 years of age, that is, beyond the age for marriage, and of proven virtue especially in regard to sexual matters, the virgins tended to be younger. Some of us probably carry from our study of the saints in grade school the notion that the typical virgin was about eleven years old! In fact, because girls married very young at that time and consecrated virgins were expected to be physically intact, the representation of virgins as very young girls was a way of emphasizing their perpetual physical virginity. Physical virginity was by no means the theological determinant of consecrated virginity, but it was assumed that the state of consecrated virginity was undertaken by actual virgins. They were generally at least 40 years of age; in some parts of the world the age requirement was lowered to 25. In other words, virginity was an adult state of life, not a way of rescuing young maidens from their father's household in early adolescence and keeping them pure like vestal virgins for the rest of their life. It was a state of life open to mature women who freely chose it.

Justin Martyr, writing not later than 110 A.D., tells us that there were in the Christian community both men and women who had lived from their adulthood, that is since their baptism, 70 years in the state of virginity. This statement locates the origin of consecrated virginity in New Testament times. These virgins did not live in groups as the widows tended to do. They ordinarily lived in their own homes within the local church community. They were known to the bishop and to the community as people who had promised their virginity to God. Virginity was a public state of life in the church. It was understood to be undertaken primarily for the sake of contemplation. In contrast to the widows, whose primary motivation seems to have been ministerial, the consecrated virgins were primarily contemplatives who did not tend as readily toward community life. We will see, as a kind of historical pattern, that there are basically two kinds of motivation for religious life. One motivation is primarily ministerial; the other primarily contemplative. (I am using the term "religious" for a variety of early forms of consecrated life in order to emphasize that they all belong to the history of religious life whether or not such forms would be recognized today as religious in the canonical sense of the term.)

As far back as the 2nd century, there was some kind of public ceremony of veiling-of-virgins. It established the person in a state of life comparable to marriage, with severe penalties for infidelity after what we would call today the profession of virginity. By the 4th century there were very elaborate and beautiful rites for the consecration of virgins which gradually, because of the problem with physical virginity as such, were replaced by vows of celibacy or chastity. This vow later was combined with other vows, e.g. poverty and obedience, and with the living of common life. By the end of the Middle Ages consecrated virginity as such ceased to exist as a state of life. In our own times, it was revived for monastics by Pius XI. Pius XII gave permission for a rite of consecration to be used for virgins living in the world.

In 1283, Boniface VIII imposed enclosure on all consecrated virgins. The original notion of enclosure goes back to the time of the fall of Rome, and was meant as a kind of protection of virgins against the encroaching barbarians, but it is well to note that it was not until the 13th century that cloister was imposed on all religious who were consecrated virgins.

In summary, two distinct groups of religious arose in the first two centuries of the Church. The widows were primarily concerned with the ministerial dimension of Christian existence, while the virgins were primarily concerned with contemplation. The former tended to live in community, the latter to live secluded in their homes. Both groups constituted a publicly recognized state of life in the Church. What they had in common was the choice of non-marriage for the sake of the Reign of God. It is important to note that consecrated non-marriage goes back to the very early Church and that the first religious were predominantly women.

B. The Second to the Fourth Century: Transition

From the 2nd to the 4th century a transition took place. It is to this period that most historians assign the origin of religious life. Gradually the asceticism involved in the renunciation of an active sexual life for the sake of God came to be seen as a kind of training for martyrdom which was a very realistic possibility in the 2nd and 3rd centuries.

By the 4th century when, under Constantine, the persecutions ended, virginity and asceticism had come to be seen as a kind of substitute for martyrdom. Martyrdom was a matter of deep concern in the early Church because it was an ever-present threat. It was interpreted theologically as the fullest possible identification with Christ. We can see this theologizing in the way the story of Stephen is told in the Acts of the Apostles. Stephen says at his martyrdom the very words that Jesus said on the Cross. His persecutors say to him the same things that were said to Jesus at his martyrdom. Stephen the martyr is presented as another Christ. This fascination with martyrdom was a profoundly spiritual phenomenon. But we also need to be aware of the close connection that this suggested between virginity, or consecrated non-marriage, and asceticism. This connection has given a certain ascetical twist to the whole notion of religious life. What started out, especially among the virgins, as a choice of non-marriage as the embodiment of a total consecration to Christ in contemplation took on a kind of ascetical tonality in this period of transition.

C. The Third to the Fifth Century: Desert Monasticism and Its Successors.

The 3rd to the 5th century is characterized by the development of desert monasticism. In the East two forms of this life developed. A form of solitary life began with Anthony of the Desert (250-356) who lived in Egypt. Around him developed two kinds of solitary life, both of which reappear in the Middle Ages. The first was a strictly solitary eremitical life. The second was a form of life in which a number of hermits lived in a kind of loosely-structured community. They came together from time to time for liturgy or for conferences with a spiritual Father or Mother, but basically they lived alone.

With Pachomius (290-346) began the development of

what is called cenobitical or community desert monasticism. Pachomius and his sister, Mary, founded a community in the desert, one branch of which was for men, and the other for women. The brother and sister gathered people together in monasteries and Pachomius wrote the first monastic rule.

Basil the Great (329-379), who lived in Syria, was a follower of Pachomius. He incorporated the notions of Pachomius into a more tightly knit form of monastic life according to the rule of St. Basil which is still lived today in the East. Basil built smaller monasteries because he wanted closer relations between superiors and subjects. He also wanted the monastery completely integrated into the life of the local Church, so rather than building out in the desert as Anthony did, he had the monastery close to the city where the religious could participate in the on-going life of the local Church. He also founded a monastery for women and still today there are women in the East who live the rule of St. Basil.

Gregory of Nazianzen (330-390), also in the Basilian tradition, wrote a very interesting treatise on virginity. Gregory considered virginity or chastity, undertaken by vow, to achieve all the benefits that life in the desert had to offer. We see here a tendency to fuse all the values sought in various kinds of consecrated life into the ideal of virginity. By the golden age of writings on virginity, the 5th century, we find virginity lauded as the quintessence of all perfection. Unfortunately, we find in much of this writing the notion that virginity is such a wonderful summing up of Christian life because it is so difficult and painful. Celibacy is understood more and more in ascetical rather than mystical terms.

Gregory of Nyssa (c. 335-394), also in the tradition of Basil, introduced another element into monastic life — the importance of study. Study remained an important element in almost all forms of religious life right up to our own times.

In summary, by the 5th century in the East both solitary and communitarian forms of religious life had developed and the first formal rules had been written. The interpretation of non-marriage for the sake of the Reign of God had become increasingly ascetical. Both total separation from and full integration into the life of the local church community were espoused by different communities, and study had become an important element in religious life. Much that was characteristic of later forms of religious life began in this period of desert monasticism in the East.

Athanasius (296-372) and Jerome (340-420), both trained in the East, transported religious life for both men and women into the Western Church. Jerome, a scholar enamored of monastic life, emphasized the importance of study. Because he could not quite separate himself from his books, he came to the conclusion that study was a good substitute for manual labor in the monastic life. He considered it just as demanding, just as purifying and ascetical, as the life of manual work.

In the West, monastic development moved in two directions: clerical and non-clerical. Eusebius of Vercelle (283-371), Ambrose (340-397), and Augustine (354-430) were leaders in the first. The form which Augustine developed, later known as the Canons Regular, involved the clergy of a diocese living a community life at the Cathedral under a rule. Augustine was interested in the development of cenobitical religious life for both men and women, but he was especially concerned for his own clerics in the diocese of Hippo.

In the non-clerical development the most important figure is John Cassian (360-435), who brought the teachings of the Eastern desert monastics to the West by his writings, particularly his *Collationes,* which became the constant reading matter for monks down to the 16th and 17th centuries. Into his work, Cassian built the sayings and teachings of the desert fathers, proof of the tremendous influence that Eastern monasticism has had on the West through one individual.

Caesarius of Arles (470-543) introduced some very important elements into the organization of a monastery. He considered it important for monks to be stable in the monastery of their profession. He also thought it important that nuns be cloistered. These cloistered women were later joined to the Carthusians and became Carthusian nuns. It was Caesarius who inaugurated a tradition of cloistered, contemplative life that would reappear much later.

In summary, during this period we see several developments in religious life. There is an increasing importance ascribed to the intellectual life; it can literally take the place of manual labor. Religious life can be either clerical or lay. There arises a new form of religious life, the Canons Regular, in which apostolic involvement, particularly the exercise of ordained ministry, is intrinsic to the life itself. They "religionize" their ministerial life instead of "ministerializing" their contemplative life. We also note during this period the introduction of stability as a monastic requirement and of cloister for ascetical reasons for women.

D. The Fifth to the Twelfth Century: Early Medieval Monasticism

The 5th to the 12th century, marked by the development of early monasticism, is often considered the classical period of religious life. This period began with Benedict (480-547) and his followers. Benedict began his religious life as a hermit and intended to continue as such, but the fame of his sanctity spread so rapidly and widely that many people came to him to be formed in the spiritual life. He yielded to their call and set up monasteries for the many who needed him, organizing a form of religious life which soon became dominant in the West and which was considered for many centuries as the standard against which any authentic form of religious life had to be judged.

People came to Benedict precisely so that he could instruct them in the interior life. Thus, he came to see the role of the abbot or abbess as absolutely essential. The monastery was defined as a community gathered around the abbot or abbess who was to be both spiritual father or mother and temporal administrator. The model here is not a monarchy with the superior as king or queen ruling subjects. The model is that of a feudal lord who protects and cares for, guides and leads, a large group which understands itself in familial terms. Because of this relationship the leader is not called a king or a general or a superior, but a father or a mother, an abbot or an abbess.

Benedict's conception of the religious community as a family has remained powerful down through the ages. Stability, for Benedict, was important. He built stability into monastic life in two ways: the abbot was to be elected for life, thus assuring internal stability in the community; the monks were to be professed for life in the monastery of their profession so that they could neither leave nor be moved around. Stability is an important value in the spiritual life, even for religious who move about for apostolic reasons. As we all know, one of the ways of escaping our spiritual problems is to keep moving and hope they do not follow us to a new location. Benedict realized that living the interior life required that one stop and face the problems. He therefore did not want his religious simply wandering about. He wanted them in a monastery where they would deal with the reason they had come there, namely, to seek God.

In the Benedictine tradition the Divine Office became the main work of the community. Liturgy, along with manual labor, was the primary work of the monk. Study also remained a very important factor in monastic life. The monastery became a self-contained local community, a social unit having in itself everything which it needed to survive. It became a self-contained economic system, and everyone within it could live from that economic system without borrowing or bringing in anything essential from the outside. In fact, monastic living became so successful that the monasteries became wealthy in every way: in terms of their spiritual life, their intellectual life, and their material life. They became sources of enrichment for the areas around them.

Benedict himself did not found a feminine branch of his order. His sister Scholastica started out as a consecrated virgin but gradually began to follow the Benedictine rule, adapted for women. Until the 12th century the only forms of feminine religious life known in the West were those which followed the Augustinian Rule and those which followed the Benedictine Rule.

This period, from the 5th to the 12th century, is then the time of the great spread of cenobitical monasticism. Benedictine monasticism played a major role in the evangelization of the "barbarians" who overran Europe during the period we came to call the Dark Ages. It became the most important single religious and cultural force in Europe. Its early medieval development, from the 5th to the 9th century, was rapid and widespread. However, as often happens in human affairs, the increasing wealth and power of the monasteries brought about a gradual decline in fervor so that by the 10th and 11th centuries there was a felt need for some very serious and thoroughgoing reform. This was the first time in the history of religious life that an order had to be reformed because it had fallen away from its first fervor. The reform began with the great experiment of Cluny, which was short-lived but very influential. The reformed monastery of Citeaux, founded in 1098, gave rise to an order which is still alive in the Church today, the Cistercians, who are Benedictines of strict observance. After the Reformation, the Cistercian monastery at La Trappe initiated further reform in the direction of severity and asceticism. The monks of this tradition are today's Trappists.

At about the same time, Romuald (950-1027) founded the Camaldolese, a cloistered eremitical branch of the Benedictines begun in Italy in 1020. The Camaldolese are still in existence in somewhat mitigated form. In fact, an interesting experiment involving the Camaldolese is going on in California today. A group of American Camaldolese monks and a group of Anglican Benedictine monks have formed a completely integrated community.Both orders come from the Benedictine tradition and they have found that their meeting at the level of monastic spirituality is much deeper than their doctrinal disunity at the denominational level.

The Carthusians were also founded at this time by St. Bruno (1030-1101). Bruno revived the cloistered contemplative tradition that began with Caesarius of Arles. The Carthusians are primarily an eremitical group which is an offshoot of the reform movement within Benedictine monasticism.

Another development in this medieval period was a refounding of the Canons Regular begun by Augustine. The Canons were clerics attached to the cathedral of the diocese who organized themselves into a kind of religious community. The first medieval rule for Canons Regular was written in 754 by Chrodegang; an even better known rule was formulated by the Council of Aix-la-Chapelle in 817. Later synods gave full canonical status to the Canons Regular, which in the 12th and 13th centuries were very powerful communities. Among the famous medieval Canons were the theologians Richard and Hugh of St. Victor. Canons Regular, although not numerous, still exist today and are undergoing an interesting revival. Some diocesan priests who feel the isolation of their life style seek a form of life determined primarily by their ordained ministry but with the support of community life. This makes the life of the Canons Regular such as the Premonstratensians attractive to young men who feel called to ordained ministry. Also, because their canonical status was established in the 11th century by church synods, the Canons Regular enjoy a singular immunity to the current canonical process for approval of rules. They can, in chapter, revise their own rules, which do not have to be approved by the Congregation for Religious and Secular Institutes. This increases their potential for growth and development in response to contemporary needs.

In summary, the medieval period saw a number of important developments in religious life. The role of the abbot became central in both eremitical and communal forms, whether lay or clerical. Also, it is interesting to note that women participated in all forms of religious life that were not essentially clerical. During this period both cloistered and apostolic forms flourished side by side. And we see the first example of a radical, thoroughgoing reform of religious life in which an order that had deteriorated did not simply die out but was renewed and brought back to its full fervor.

E. The Thirteenth Century: The Development of the Mendicant Movement

The 13th century is marked by the development of the mendicant orders. The two great founders of this period are Francis of Assisi (1182-1226) and Dominic Guzman (1170-1221). Today, Franciscans, Dominicans, Carmelites, and Servites among others carry on this great medieval tradition.

In view of the development of religious life up to the middle ages, the mendicant orders represent a very original departure from tradition. They abandoned the ideal of stability which dated from the 4th century. In these new orders religious did not profess stability in one monastery; rather they became members of the order as a whole and therefore could be moved around among the various houses of the order for the purpose of apostolic works. It is important to note that in this new movement apostolic involvement became an important determinant of the form of religious life. In the adaptation, the mendicants did retain certain elements of monastic life such as the conventual liturgy, i.e. Eucharist and the Divine Office in common. But they considered the essential of their life to be what they called "apostolic life", i.e. a life of living and preaching the Gospel. Also interesting to note is the transformation of the religious community from a self-contained economic unit, as was the monastery, to a participant in the economic situation that was emerging in the Middle Ages. In tune with the rise of the middle class, the emergence of the university, and the development of city life, the mendicants became wage earners of a sort. They were either beggars supporting themselves by alms or they lived from what they made from their work. Medieval society was very different from the feudal society in which Benedictine monasticism was born. The mendicants became somewhat interdependent with the surrounding society, developing an urban form of religious life closely associated with the universities and devoted to preaching and evangelization.

In one sense, the mendicants developed a more democratic form of religious life than the Benedictines. The chapter, which was on-going, and which met daily or weekly, became the ordinary way in which affairs were conducted in the orders. Francis called the superiors in his order "ministers", that is, servants. They were neither monarchs nor patriarchs but servants of the community.

Mendicant orders had women members whose communities were called "second orders." The "first order" members were men, mostly clerics; the "second order" members were women who by this time were cloistered. Finally, "third orders" were founded whose members made private vows and followed a rule suitable for people living in secular circumstances rather than in convents or monasteries. Some very famous third order women, such as Catherine of Siena (1347-1380) and Rose of Lima (1586-1617), are generally viewed by tradition as religious. Juridically they were not, but theologically they were. Had they been members of the second order, that is, canonical religious, they would have been cloistered and unable to carry out the ministries for which they are so revered. This probably represents the first successful feminine out-maneuvering of male restrictions for the sake of apostolic involvement.

In the High Middle Ages another interesting form of religious life developed. Its members were called Beguines and the movement was especially strong in the Low Countries. An outstanding representative of the Beguine movement was Hadewijch of Antwerp who wrote between 1230-1250. The Beguine movement was tributary to the powerful spiritual movements of the High Middle Ages but it was also a response to the social and political situation of the times. Many of the Beguines were women whose husbands were off on the crusades or who had lost their husbands in the "holy wars." These women chose to live the evangelical counsels within communes, sometimes in individual houses, sometimes in communities. It was understood that they could leave at any time if they chose to marry or if their husbands returned, but the simple and celibate lifestyle was actually chosen as a means to contemplative prayer. The Beguines were not totally unlike some non-canonical communities developing today and this has led to a renewed interest in this medieval movement. The Beguines retained their own property but with a strong commitment to simplicity of life. Because it was a feminine form of life which had no male counterpart, the Beguine movement has suffered the fate of most female developments, namely, erasure from history. We are just beginning to get some serious studies of this movement.

In summary, some developments of particular note in this period are the following: the beginning of the development of a mobile as opposed to a stable form of religious life; religious working for a living in the larger society rather than running their own economic systems separate from the rest of society; the combination of monastic and apostolic life with emphasis on the apostolic dimension; Third Orders developing as a form of religious life that would allow people, especially women, to exercise an apostolate outside the religious cloister; and the Beguines, who represent a kind of commitment that is theologically very close to religious life, but does not involve most of the elements usually considered essential, such as public vows, mandatory common life, superiors, habit, cloister, or necessarily permanent commitment.

F. The Fourteenth to the Sixteenth Century:
Development Among Women Religious and Clerics

Although male religious life was in decline during the 14th and 15th centuries, interesting developments occurred among women devoted to the consecrated life. As already noted, the Beguines, whose movement began in the 12th century and reached its peak in the 14th century, were women without religious vows who nevertheless led in community lives devoted to prayer and good works. Anchoresses, such as Juliana of Norwich (1342-after 1416), were consecrated virgins living in solitude lives of intense contemplation. Catherine of Siena (1347-1380) was a third order Dominican who, without public vows of religion, combined high mysticism with profound involvement in social and political life. The

14th and 15th centuries are studded with brilliant and holy women, members of a variety of forms of life which were theologically, if not juridically, religious.

The 16th century was dominated by the Protestant Reformation and the Catholic Counter-Reformation. During this period Teresa of Avila (1515-1582) reformed the female branch of the Carmelites, restoring this form of cloistered contemplative religious life to its original fervor. She guided her younger contemporary, John of the Cross (1542-1591), in the reformation of the male branch of the order.

But, as the Carmelites were returning to their earlier cloistered form and fervor, a new form of religious life, the Clerics Regular, was emerging. Unlike the Canons, who lived a semi-monastic community life, the Clerics Regular were communities of priests who, in order to carry out their apostolic work, gave up conventual liturgy, i.e., Eucharist and Divine Office in common, most elements of common life, and distinctive garb. The Jesuits were, and remain, the largest and most influential group of Clerics Regular. Although at the time this form of religious life was shocking in its abandonment of most of the distinguishing characteristics of monasticism, it has had a major influence on the development of contemporary apostolic religious life. Two major contributions of this new form to later religious life were the centrality assigned to mission and the novel institution of simple rather than solemn vows. While solemn vows entailed cloister, simple vows admitted of some flexibility. The 1983 revision of Canon Law abolished the juridical distinction between the two kinds of profession, but prior to Vatican II, the distinction was of the greatest practical importance, especially for women.

Although cloister was imposed on all women who were juridically religious and most women religious accepted the restriction, many creative and committed women in the 16th century found ways to circumvent this impediment to apostolic activity. For example, Angela Merici (1474-1540) founded her Company of St. Ursula whose members practiced poverty, virginity and obedience but who were not canonically religious, to revitalize family life through religious education. Mary Ward (1586-1646) founded the Institute of Mary, a community of women who were uncloistered, without habit, and committed to apostolic mobility. Though her Institute was suppressed in 1631 and she herself imprisoned, the Institute was finally approved in 1877. Her rule became a model both for apostolic congregations of later centuries and for lay apostolic groups such as the Grail. Vincent de Paul (1581-1660) founded the Daughters of Charity who, not having public vows, were uncloistered and thus able to participate in the works of charity for which they have become renowned.

Another apostolic route around the restrictions of cloister consisted in bringing those in need into the religious house to receive medical assistance, education, or other forms of ministry. In short, despite the restrictions cloister placed on those who were canonically religious, committed women founded and participated in numerous forms of apostolic life which would not be recognized as religious life until the 20th century.

G. *The Seventeenth to the Twentieth Century:*
Congregations of Simple Vows

Following the lead of the Jesuits who initiated the practice of simple profession, a number of men founded clerical groups, such as the Redemptorists, the Vincentians, the Passionists, and the Salesians, whose members made simple rather than solemn vows. Other men formed non-clerical religious congregations such as the Brothers of the Christian Schools and the Xaverian Brothers. Unlike the lay brothers who were founded in the 11th century as servant members of clerical orders, these new lay orders of men were male counterparts to apostolic women's congregations. Finally, some men joined together in communities, such as the Sulpicians, Columbans, and Maryknoll missionaries, whose members made promises or commitments but no vows.

While the male orders, both clerical and lay, tended to retain much monastic practice, women's communities of this same period tended away from monastic and toward apostolic forms of life. This development was actually fostered by the social chaos that followed the French Revolution and the anti-clericalism characteristic of the rising national states in Europe. By this time habits and cloister were impediments to meeting the vast and pressing human needs for health care, social services, and education. Religiously committed women answered these needs and went on to help evangelize the new world and educate a new kind of citizen for democratic participation.

The new congregations of apostolic religious women such as the Sisters of Mercy, the Religious of the Sacred Heart, the Sisters, Servants of the Immaculate Heart of Mary, the Religious of the Sacred Heart of Mary and many others were finally recognized as canonical religious congregations of simple vows by the document *Conditae a Christo* of Leo XIII in 1900. It is important to note that most of the apostolic congregations of women were founded in the 1800's, almost a century before this form of life was recognized as religious. In other words, vows and common life were ordered to mission, rather than mission being a simple overflow of monastic life. These new congregations, founded for and ordered to the apostolate, attracted large numbers of young women even before they were officially recognized. There is very little in the literature of this period to suggest that these women did not consider themselves religious.

By the late 19th century the apostolic congregations of simple vows had become the dominant form of women's religious life. In the 20th century Pius XII recognized a new form of consecrated life, the Secular Institute. From the very beginning the distinction between canonical religious life and the Secular Institutes was less than clear. But since Vatican II and the renewal of apostolic religious life even such notes as habit and common life have ceased to distinguish religious from their sisters in Secular Institutes. The 1983 revision of Canon Law assimilates the two forms under the heading "Institutes of Consecrated Life."

Finally, since the Council, a new form of consecrated life

has developed. These non-canonical communities, such as the Sisters for Christian Community, are emerging very rapidly. Over 400 such communities already exist. Their members make perpetual private vows of celibacy, poverty and obedience, and devote themselves completely to ministry. Their non-canonical condition protects them from Vatican surveillance and control without, it seems, in any way limiting their commitment or ministerial effectiveness. At the present time the non-canonical communities are the fastest growing form of vowed life and, though not canonically religious, there is little or nothing of theological significance to distinguish their members from religious or members of Secular Institutes.

The non-canonical communities symbolized the growing ambivalence of religious, particularly women, toward unilateral regulation by male ecclesiastical authority. While women religious appreciate the advantages of public recognition by the Church, they are increasingly unwilling to submit to non-dialogical regulation of their lives by men who do not share their life experience. Such regulation is coming to be experienced as personally degrading and ministerially disruptive. Furthermore, for theological and social reasons, many religious are beginning to question the value of some elements of the "publicity" of their lives, such as special dress, special housing, and "religious" employment arrangements. Finally, religious women have begun to reflect theologically on the ministerial dimension of their lives and have come to realize that ministry is intrinsic to their form of religious life. The centrality of ministry does not compete with, but flows from, their religious consecration, and the arbitary limitation or suppression of ministries in the name of theoretical and abstract "essential elements" of religious life cannot be accepted. What began as a spontaneous religious response to human need is now experienced as a Gospel imperative intrinsic to and constitutive of apostolic religious life.

III. CONCLUSIONS

Let us now draw two conclusions from this much-too-rapid and incomplete survey of the development of religious life. First, the tendency of historians and church officials to regard male forms of religious life as paradigmatic and female forms as derivative and dependent is unjustified. Women's religious life is both older and more varied than men's and has not been affected by the clericalizing influence that has at times retarded change and development among men.

Secondly, when all the data is examined, it is clear that there are really only two constants in the history of religious life. The first is that religious life, whatever form it took, was always regarded by its members and others as a "state of life," a recognizable and permanent phenomenon in the Church's life. The second, closely related to the first, is that religious life as a state of life, has always been characterized and constituted by the permanent commitment to non-marriage for the sake of the Reign of God.

Apart from those two constants, there has been immense variety among and within the forms of religious life. Religious life has been solitary or communitarian and the latter sometimes, not always, involved common life. Religious have lived secluded from the world, in their families, or immersed in secular life. Religious vows have been public and private, and at times there have been no vows at all. Some forms of religious life are monarchical, others familial, and still others democratic. Some Orders have professed stability while for others mobility is a constitutive virtue. The relation of communities to the local church has varied from almost total separation to near total immersion. Groups of religious have worn habits and others have not; some have been cloistered and others not; for some manual work took precedence over intellectual work while for others the reverse was true. There are contemplative forms of religious life and active forms. Some religious have lived in self-supporting monasteries, and others have been itinerant beggars, and still others supported themselves with paid labor.

This does not exhaust the list of variations but attending to this enormous variety should make us cautious about identifying any of these developments as "essential elements of religious life." History helps us to realize that God alone is absolute.

Lecture II:
Trends and Patterns
in the History of Religious Life

I. INTRODUCTION

In the previous lecture, I tried to sketch the history of religious life from New Testament times to the present day, and to draw some conclusions from that survey. The primary conclusion was that the form of religious life has varied enormously in the course of 2000 years of development. In this lecture, I want to return to this historical material in order to try to discern some trends and patterns in the development which might contribute to our reflection on religious life today.

First, by means of Chart I, entitled "Emergence of Forms of Religious Life," let us trace the pattern of development. As can be seen, there are two streams of development. It is difficult to assign appropriate names to the two branches but in broad terms the first branch includes those forms of religious life which developed primarily in response to a call to a lifestyle of consecrated celibacy, whereas the second branch includes those forms which grew out of a primarily ascetical or apostolic call. Obviously, the distinction is inadequate because the widows of New Testament times were deeply involved in ministry and the consecrated virgins of the monastic tradition were less ascetically than mystically oriented. However, I think the chart gives a rough idea of how various forms of religious life evolved.

Chart I

EMERGENCE OF FORMS OF RELIGIOUS LIFE

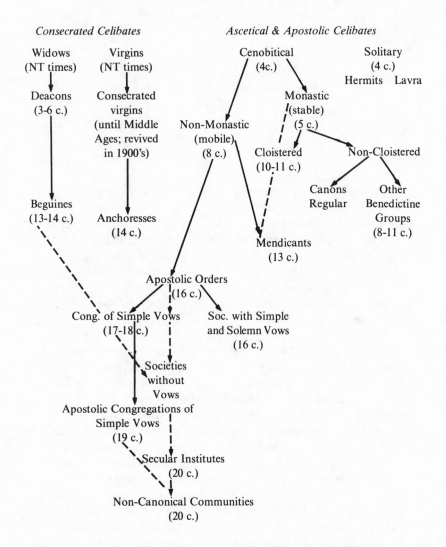

Consecrated Celibates

Ascetical & Apostolic Celibates

Widows
(NT times)

Virgins
(NT times)

Cenobitical
(4c.)

Solitary
(4 c.)
Hermits   Lavra

Deacons
(3-6 c.)

Consecrated
virgins
(until Middle
Ages; revived
in 1900's)

Non-Monastic
(mobile)
(8 c.)

Monastic
(stable)
(5 c.)

Cloistered
(10-11 c.)

Non-Cloistered

Beguines
(13-14 c.)

Anchoresses
(14 c.)

Canons
Regular

Other
Benedictine
Groups
(8-11 c.)

Mendicants
(13 c.)

Apostolic Orders
(16 c.)

Cong. of Simple Vows
(17-18 c.)

Soc. with Simple
and Solemn Vows
(16 c.)

Societies
without
Vows

Apostolic Congregations of
Simple Vows
(19 c.)

Secular Institutes
(20 c.)

Non-Canonical Communities
(20 c.)

Secondly, it is important for us to see how religious today are distributed in terms of religious life forms. The 1982 statistics were the most recent available to me. According to these official statistics there are 1,190,272 religious in the world of whom 229,181 are men and 960,991 are women. In the United States there are 151,822 religious of whom 30,452 are men and 121,370 are women. There are, therefore, nearly four women religious for every male religious; about one of every seven women religious is American; and the vast majority of male religious (178,763 out of 259,733) are clerics.

Chart II

Current (1982) Statistics on Religious

A. World religious population

Religious Men	229,281
-Clerical	(156,191)
-Lay	(73,090)
Religious Women	960,991

B. U.S.A: religious population

Religious Men	30,452
-Clerical	(22,572)
-Lay	(7,880)
Religious Women	121,370

If we look at the distribution of the world's religious by form (statistics available from 1968) we find the following:

Chart III

Distribution (1968) of Roman Catholic Religious

Type	Century of Origin	Men	Women
Monastics	5-6th c.	20,000 (7%)	14,000 (1%)
Mendicants	10-13 c.	75,000 (25%)	36,000 (3%)
Clerics Regular	16 c.	42,000 (14%)	
Congregations of Simple Vows	17-18 c.	30,000 (10%)	45,000 (5%)
Congregations of Simple Vows	19 c.	109,000 (42%)	791,000 (91%)
Secular Institutes	20 c.	Over 50,000?	
Non-Canonical Communities	20 c.	Over 400 Groups?	

Obviously, these absolute numbers would be considerably smaller today because of the significant decrease in numbers of religious since 1968. However, the proportions are probably roughly the same except for the sharper decline in the numbers of religious brothers compared to other categories of religious.

These statistics suggest certain important conclusions: (1) Religious life is an overwhelmingly female phenomenon; (2) The vast majority of religious belong to a tradition which dates back only to the 19th century. In the light of these conclusions, it is not difficult to see why women religious are the primary agents of change in religious life today, and why they are impatient with attempts to "monasticize" their life or relegate their ministries to secondary status.

II. TRENDS AND PATTERNS

With this background and information, we turn to some trends and patterns which can be discerned in the history of religious life. One pattern which is very important for us today is the relationship that has always obtained between a given form of religious life and, on the one hand, the socio-economic conditions of society at the time that this form emerged, and on the other, the ecclesial situation of the time. Both factors form part of the context for the emergence of a particular form of religious life.

A. Developments up to the Twentieth Century

In the earliest period, that of the *widows and virgins*, a very pure form of religious life arose. It had no prehistory. It was a mature response to the Gospel call for self-dedication to Christ and to the needs of the newly-born Christian community. We should be aware that these new forms of life, that is, institutionalized states of unmarried life for Christian women, served another very important function in a pagan society in which a young virgin or widow had no alternative except patriarchal marriage. If the husband in question was pagan, the possibility of her being able to live a truly Christian life would be minimal. Perhaps, had Christian women had other options during this earliest period, fewer would have chosen consecrated virginity or widowhood. This hypothesis in no way undermines the reality and fervor of early religious commitment; it is simply a realistic appraisal of the relationship between socio-economic context and the development of the earliest forms of religious life.

Desert Monasticism of the 4th century was likewise closely related to ecclesial and secular contexts. After the Edict of Milan (313) the Church ceased to be a socially oppressed and persecuted group. Some fervent Christians felt that the liberated Church of this period was becoming too acculturated and secularized and that the only way to resist this spiritual apostasy was to seek in the desert the exclusion and suffering which had once been the societal fate of all Christians. Furthermore, as actual martyrdom became a less imminent threat, many fervent Christians sought a kind of spiritual martyrdom in asceticism. The development of desert monasticism with its flight from the secular world and its extreme asceticism was a practical implementation of such convictions. Today the asceticism of the desert appears harsh and negative. However, it was not unrelated to Greek philosophical thought of the period which prompted intense physical discipline and purification as a necessary preparation for contemplation. In other words, desert monasticism was not something that came from heaven in pure form; it was a response to the situation in the Church of the time and drew many of its ideals and practices from the intellectual milieu of the hellenistic world.

Monasticism, as we have seen, was socially a feudal form of life. This is not surprising since it emerged in a feudal society. Early medieval religious life was closely modeled on the existing form of social organization. Monasticism developed at a time when foreign hordes were overrunning Europe and when classical culture was falling apart. There was need for places of learning, sanctuaries for culture, where what was left of the Golden Age of Greece and Rome could be preserved. At the same time there was need to evangelize the pagans who were invading Europe. Here too the form of religious life was closely related to what was going on in the Church and surrounding society.

In the High Middle Ages when the *mendicants and the Canons Regular* emerged, society was becoming progressively urban. This was the time of the rise of the cities, the foundation of the great universities, the rise of the middle class, and the emergence of a poorer class who were virtually serfs. There was a need for an evangelization of the cities and an evangelization of the country folk who were not part of urban society. As Aristotelian philosophy revitalized intellectual life, a Christian synthesis of philosophy and theology was sought, as was a reinterpretation of Christian doctrine in terms that could be understood by educated people of the time. Here again, we see the intimate connection between the development of religious life and the social, cultural and intellectual developments in Church and society.

The *Clerics Regular* are an even clearer example of this interrelationship. The Church in the 16th century was under siege from the Protestant Reformation. It experienced a need for an intelligent, informed, committed defense against the heretics. The Church also needed a profound reform of the clergy. Abuses by the clergy were a major factor in the scandals which were part of the cause for the Reformation. At the same time the Church also had to do something about the new lands which were being discovered, especially by the Spaniards. And so a form of religious life was inaugurated whose members were devoted to the spreading of the faith in the newly discovered lands and to defending the faith in Europe. The Society of Jesus was founded at a time when, for the first time in 1500 years, the central authority of the Church was threatened from within the Western World. This dedicated band of religious swore allegiance to the Holy See and went out to do battle with paganism and heresy.

The *congregations of simple vows* also arose in response to ecclesial and cultural challenge, at a time of tremendous social and cultural upheaval in Europe. Vast populations were devastated by continuous warfare. The secular clergy was uneducated and largely unable to attend to the needs of a chaotic society. All the disorder that followed in the wake of revolution — plagues, sickness, orphans in need of homes and instruction, desperate religious needs — called for a new kind of religious life. Congregations of simple vows were founded to meet these needs in society. In many cases these apostolic congregations were founded to meet the needs of the New World. The Catholic immigrants who came to our own country from various nations in Europe founded "ghetto churches" which were not well integrated into the larger protestant society. It is not surprising that religious orders founded in this setting tended to be "ghetto" groups which saw themselves as living a private and secret life in an enclave untouched by, and indeed hostile to, everything outside itself. The religious congregations ministered to a Church which was brought up to be fearful of anything Protestant or American, indeed anything outside of the Catholic "world." As a result these congregations represented a kind of ghettoized religious life, serving a ghettoized Catholic community in the New World.

Another factor in the 19th century world and Church which influenced the development of religious life was the opening to evangelization of the African continent and the Far East. The need for missionaries to these new areas of evangelization was great. During this period came the foundation of the Maryknoll Sisters and the Medical Mission Sisters. In short, the 19th century developments in religious life, like those of earlier centuries, were very much a response to the ecclesial and societal conditions of the times.

B. Twentieth Century Developments

In our own time, the 20th century, certain characteristics of society and Church are influencing religious life, just as surrounding contexts influenced religious life in earlier periods. However, because of the revolutions in both science and the media, cultural change today takes place much faster and at greater depth than it did in times past. Furthermore, Vatican II's affirmation of the Church's integration into the world as well as the integration of American Catholics into the mainstream of American society has made a "ghetto" form of religious life no longer viable. Both of these factors — the rate and depth of change and the emergence of the Church from its post-Tridentine siege mentality and defensiveness — should lead us to expect that the developments in contemporary religious life will be more rapid, more profound, and more original than developments in earlier times.

Let us look briefly at some of the major developments in 20th century Church and society which have had a major impact on recent developments in religious life.

First, we might note the professionalization of American society. We have become a competence-oriented society, and competence is established by credentials. The days are gone when an uneducated and inexperienced 19-year old could be turned overnight into a high school calculus teacher by edict of the superior. Far-seeing religious who recognized this development founded the Sister Formation Conference in the 1950's to insure the proper professional preparation of apostolic religious without which they would not be able to carry on effective ministries in American society.

A second important cultural factor is democratization. The near universality of education in the United States makes citizens participants in processes which affect them. To try to run a monarchical operation in the Church has become increasingly difficult, whether at the level of the parish, diocese, or religious community. It is increasingly difficult for Americans to accept the notion of a divine-right monarch who is appointed directly by God. Continuous repetition of claims to unaccountable authority has had less and less real effect on Americans who have moved, from cultural experience, to asking not "Who said it?" but "Is it true?" If people strongly suspect that what is being said is not true, repeating it in a louder voice does not make it more convincing. The reaction in 1968 to *Humanae Vitae* is a good example of this phenomenon. Democratization is a powerful trend in American religious life and probably the one which causes most alarm in Vatican circles. But it is virtually impossible for American religious who espouse participation, communication, accountability, and shared authority in every other sphere of experience to accept hierarchy as the appropriate form of organization for religious life.

A third important cultural force influencing religious life today is feminism, which involves a fundamental rejection of male domination and a basic affirmation of the equality of women with men. The majority of American religious are women and all of the Church's official representatives are men. As increasing numbers of women become feminists, the male domination of women in the Church becomes increasingly unacceptable. To say, "In faith, try to put that aside and concentrate on the fact that they are ordained" not only does not help, it exacerbates the situation, for clericalism involves an elitist superiority which is no more acceptable in the Church than analogous forms of elitist expertise are in society. We are beginning to question doctors, dentists, lawyers and teachers. We no longer say, "The doctor said . . ." but rather, "I think I'll get a second opinion." If we do not like the work a professional is doing, or if that professional does not have the time to explain to us what he or she is doing, we feel free to say, "I'll deal with someone else." Americans are less and less willing to turn over major segments of their lives, including religion, to the professional "elites." We use experts as resource people, but we do not abdicate our responsibility to these people. The equivalent of elitist expertise in the religious sphere is clericalism. At its height it elicited the "Ask Father" syndrome. Few American Catholics, and even fewer educated religious, are any longer afflicted with this syndrome. Male dominance and clericalism are being rejected in the 20th century Church and this rejection cannot fail to influence religious life, especially that of women.

A fourth factor influencing religious life today is our sense of the global situation, our participation in the world scene. It is virtually impossible for us to think exclusively in terms of "our" parish or "our" congregation or even "our" nation.

Most religious can recall the days when they did not know anybody outside their own congregation. Today, many would probably say that some of their best friends are people not in their own congregations, even people who are not in religious life. These broader contacts have effectively undermined the closed sociology of knowledge which made religious ready and able to accept as true whatever was promulgated in their own group. Today religious read newspapers, watch television, mix with "outsiders," and in general, have a larger frame of reference for judging the validity of what is promulgated by Church or congregation. They are more critical, in a good sense. But they are also less "manageable." This is a major factor in the difficulties between American religious and the Vatican. Things do not become acceptable simply because they are "official." They also have to be demonstrably true, reasonable, and likely to promote more good than harm.

Finally, issues of global justice have become very important for religious who are beginning to ask where their investments are going, whom they are supporting. In the past, most religious did not even know how much money the congregation had or who had control of it. Now they want to know how much there is, where it is going, and who is making decisions. This is only one example of how increasing realization of the interconnectedness of justice issues affects the lives of religious. One cannot struggle for justice in one area of life and be blind to injustices in others. The Pope's recent exhortation to struggle for the elimination of all forms of oppression based on sex, coupled with his defense of discrimination against women in the Church based on divine revelation, makes no sense to people whose consciousness has been formed by justice concerns.

We could easily bring up other characteristics of the 20th century which influence religious life today. My point is that our form of life, like forms in the past, has developed in interdependence with the society and the Church in which we live. Religious life has almost always operated out of a fundamental acceptance of the basic societal situation in which it found itself, whether that meant accepting the values of feudalism in the Dark Ages, the values of urban life in the Medieval period, the ideal of conquering the world for Christ in the Counter Reformation epoch, the value of societal care in the Post-Revolution era, or the ghetto mentality of 19th century American Catholicism.

We can challenge this cultural involvement, or we can defend it. What we cannot do is deny it. This means that the theory that certain forms of religious life are eternally valid because they are realizations of some quasi-Platonic essence which has been divinely revealed is simply not true. The various forms of religious life developed in historical periods because of historical situations lived by historical people. Religious life did not come down from some mythical mount of revelation to be clothed anew in each era. Religious life is not an essence; it is a movement. If anything is of the "essence" of religious life, it is its profoundly historical character.

Having affirmed the historical embeddedness of religious life, however, I think it is necessary both to challenge and to defend this cultural involvement. This may be especially important today. We must challenge it because it is easy to be completely co-opted by our culture, to take over the values of our society uncritically and unquestioningly so that, in effect, we have nothing prophetic to say in our situation. But on the other hand, if we do not talk the same language as our contemporaries, it does not matter how important the witness we give is because it will not be heard. There are societies in which strangeness or oddity is a sign of relation to divinity. There are societies in which certain physical abnormalities or psychological aberrations are regarded as special divine marks on a child, who then grows up to be a religious figure in the group. Our society is not one of these. Simply being strange does not increase the credibility of our message. In other words, we must challenge societal values which are inhuman or unchristian but, at the same time, we must be able to communicate. We no longer live in a ghetto where a private language is understood by the initiates. If we want to talk to anybody but ourselves, we must learn the language of our contemporaries.

III. LINES OF DEVELOPMENT INTERIOR TO RELIGIOUS LIFE

We are now in a position to ask if there are any observable lines of development in this history of religious life which we have sketched.   One clearly visible trend is the movement from total physical separation from the world which began with desert monasticism to a deep involvement in the world. Vatican II, speaking of the Church from which religious life draws its identity, declared that solidarity with all the people of the world was the vocation of the Christian. Most religious can remember a time when the ultimate condemnation of any attitude, behavior, desire, relationship, or object was to designate it as "worldly." We no longer use that terminology because it is not very compatible with our conciliar ideals of solidarity with all people and salvific integration into the human enterprise. Nevertheless, what was expressed materially by actual flight from the city is a value which every form of religious life has seen the need to incorporate, namely, that there must be some kind of difference, even contrast, between religious life and the society within which it lives and witnesses. The earliest religious fled into the desert. The monastery was an area walled off from the rest of the world. Later, the walls came down but religious developed practices and wore clothes that were so different from those of society that there was a kind of psychological separation from other people. Today, we are wont to speak of cultural separation, countercultural witness. We are still in the process of searching for a way to express the value that religious assign to resisting total cultural assimilation. But we have come very far from interpreting this conviction as a call to abandon or repudiate our fellow human beings or to refuse to associate with them.

A second line of development in religious life is from solitary to communitarian forms. There are still some completely solitary religious, but the dominant form of religious life has tended to be communitarian. There are reasons for this development. Solitude is a value in all forms of religious life, but if it becomes the central value, it makes the practice of a Christian life very problematic. The practice of charity, to be realistic, usually demands some contact with others; the active exercise of the apostolate tends to call people to community; and liturgical life is impossible in solitude. The realization that community is essential to christian life and that few people can realize community without some contact with people has led to a dematerialization and interiorization of the value of solitude. Physical solitude has become a periodic intensification of interiority rather than a form of religious life.

A third development is the movement from stable to more mobile forms of religious life. Again, stability is an important religious value fostering constancy and perseverance. We all have a tendency to run away from the deepest problems of the interior life by trying to put distance between ourselves and the problematic situations. Monastic stability was a safeguard against that tendency. But in apostolic congregations stability gradually came to mean perseverance in the congregation rather than physical habitation in one house. Perseverance in the spiritual life is no less a value today than it was in earlier times. However, it has been dematerialized to some extent. While we cannot grow up in Christ if we run away from the challenges of the interior or apostolic life, change and mobility are values to us, not dangers. We face the challenge of how to realize in our time the value of fidelity in a context of continual change.

A fourth line of development is the movement from a perfection-and-salvation dominated definition of religious life toward a transformation definition. Most religious grew up with the notion of perfection as a definite goal toward which one climbed fervently hoping to reach it before death. Menologies were written to suggest that our forebears in religion attained perfection early in their religious careers and then continued on that plateau until they expired in the odor of sanctity. Today that static ideal of perfection as a definable state to be achieved seems unreal. We evaluate life itself differently, prizing change as the very heart of development. We hope to keep growing until we draw our last breath. In short, our understanding of religious life is considerably more dynamic than were earlier conceptions, and growth seems more important than perfection.

A fifth line of development in the history of religious life concerns types of organization. We traced the development from solitary forms of life through familial forms in which authority was parental to more democratic forms in the Middle Ages to the extremely hierarchical and monarchical forms of Post-Tridentine religious life. Today there is a movement away from hierarchical toward more participative forms. The will of God is no longer equated with bell, rule, or edict of the superior. Many religious view the mediation of God's will as much more complex, involving personal and societal factors as well as community structures. The purely hierarchical organization of religious life has become very problematic for many religious who see participative forms of community life as not only more human but also as more evangelical.

Finally, there is a marked trend away from male hegemony to more equal relationships and functional mutuality between men and women. This development is having profound effects on women's religious life. Fifty years ago, women simply accepted that men spoke for God in relationship to women. Many religious no longer accept this and their redefinition of male-female relations is causing serious strains in their relationships with a male-dominated Church.

In looking at these trends or lines of development in the history of religious life (and these are certainly not the only trends), we note something very important. In each case we are dealing with a genuine value. When religious first saw the importance of a particular value for religious life, the tendency was to achieve it in a very material, even physical, way. We have all experienced this tendency in our personal lives. For example, we might make a resolution such as "I will improve my prayer life. I will pray every morning for one hour." The first move is to embody the value in a practice of some kind which can be measured by the clock, or written in one's journal. But eventually, if the value is to be truly internalized, it must be transformed from a predominantly physical element of life into an interior disposition which usually gives rise to a variety of external expressions. The developments and trends in the history of religious life represent not a repudiation of values but an interiorization of them. Solitude, silence, community, obedience, stability are all religious values. But as we try to incorporate them into our lives, we see the problems with their concrete material realization and so tend to raise questions about how we can preserve the value without necessarily preserving a rigid embodiment of it.

IV. THE SUCCESSION OF PARADIGMATIC FORMS OF RELIGIOUS LIFE

I would like now to turn to the work of Lawrence Cada and his associates, published in a book called *Shaping the Coming of Age of Religious Life* (1979). These researchers have studied the historical data on the development of religious life and have discovered a pattern that can be very illuminating for us today. They point out in their study that each age has produced a new form of religious life peculiarly suited to that time. Consequently, the new form was immensely attractive to the people of the time and tended to draw many candidates to religious life. The desert became over populated in the 3rd and 4th centuries. Benedict's monasticism attracted droves of Christians from the 5th century on and, as a result, great monasteries sprang up all over Europe. The mendicant development in the Middle Ages was no less phenomenal. By the end of Francis' own lifetime, there were thousands of Franciscans. The same was true of the Jesuit development in the 16th century and of apostolic communities in the 1950's and 1960's. Today the non-canonical communities are attracting higher numbers of candidates.

In each period a new form of religious life has arisen, not without struggle and opposition. As the new form gained ascendancy it became the paradigmatic form. Often, older forms come to be seen as hold-overs from an earlier age and sometimes even as anachronisms. When they arise, new forms are almost always contested, usually for theological reasons. There is a conviction that something essential to religious life is being lost. The mendicants, roaming about like vagabonds, did not seem to realize the essential value of stability. And the Jesuits, who did not meet for common liturgy, obviously did not appreciate the essential role of community life. And then there were religious who did not wear habits; how were they going to give public witness in the world? In the 19th century there were women out of the cloister; was not cloister part of the very definition of religious life for women?

The objections were always, on the surface, theological. But underneath (and here the hermeneutics of suspicion must come into play) the new form visibly threatened the social position or power of some persons or groups in Church or society. The story of the mendicant movement is an especially good example of this dynamic. But of greater interest to us today is the male interest in women's subordination which is threatened by women religious who will not dress as they are told, live where and how they are told, nor minister only by permission. The form of religious life emerging among women today is criticized theologically as lacking certain "essential elements" of religious life, notably adequate public identification and hierarchical forms of government. But it is important to recognize the role of instant visibility and sacralized power structures in the control of people. Women religious are developing forms of religious life in which control is minimized if not eliminated and this is very threatening to those men in the Church who have a vested interest in the subordination and control of women. A new form of religious life is arising today and we can expect it to face the same difficulties that other new forms faced in the past.

As new forms arose, what happened to older forms? As young people were attracted to the new forms, the older ones tended to stabilize numerically. They usually incorporated enough of the new to remain vital, but tended to cease expanding. Those which did not adapt at all usually became museum pieces or disappeared altogether.

The pattern of growth and decline that Fitz and Cada outline in their study is as follows. First there is the period of *foundation* in which a charismatic individual or individuals who are peculiarly in tune with their times conceive the project of a new kind of evangelical life. Many such movements start but evaporate after a short time. The ones we know about are the ones that worked, the ones that somehow fit their times and took root.

Once the successful foundation is made, there is the period of *expansion*. Many people come to join the new movement and the charism is institutionalized. At this point it becomes possible to say: "Yes, this is what this group is all about. If you want to join it, this is what will be asked of you. We can now teach you what it means to be a Franciscan, a Sister of Mercy, or a Jesuit." Growth is usually, but not always, rapid during the period of expansion.

Following expansion, there is the period of *stabilization*. A social structure is in place which involves stable offices and roles. People in the congregation are related to each other in stable ways, and behaviors are ordered and standardized. There is clarity about work and purposes. The group knows how to prepare people for membership. It knows what it is about, what it is trying to do, and how to do it. Formation consists essentially in transmitting a myth that constitutes what we might call the "spirit of the group." I am using the term "myth" in the positive sense of a view of reality which embraces all of life in a meaningful, coherent way. Most religious can remember being initiated into the community myth. One knew what each stage meant, what behaviors were appropriate, which songs to sing in certain circumstances, which feasts were special and how each was celebrated. The myth and customs embraced all of life from the day one entered the postulate until one was buried in the manner prescribed and written up in the characteristic literary form of the community menology. Living the myth led to a great sense of cohesion and unity, meaningfulness and order in life. The myth and its customs could be transmitted from generation to generation. The people in charge of forming the younger generation knew what the next generation was being formed to and how to bring about that formation. Much of the formation was done by persuasion and by the indirect coercion of social pressures which is the way any social system operates. The period of stabilization is a very comfortable time because *esprit de corps* is usually high. The group has strong identity, purpose, and values. Belonging to a group during the period of stabilization gives coherence and meaning to life and one is usually willing to give one's all for the common cause.

Following this period of stabilization comes a period which most of us have already lived through, which Fitz and Cada call a period of *decline*. I do not know if that is the best word for it. It is a time not unlike middle age which someone described as the experience of becoming "unglued." Some people in the congregation begin to see a lack of fit between the theory and practice of the congregation on the one hand and the world around them on the other. Someone begins to wonder aloud why religious at a convention do not eat with their lay colleagues, especially since so much important business is done at meals. The person asks, "Why are we doing this?" and someone answers: "Because we have always done it." The implication is that all parts of the community myth and ritual are divinely instituted. But more and more members of the group begin to question the relationship of various elements of the life to sanctity and mission. With a realization of the lack of cultural fit, the theory begins to suffer some strain. Doubts arise where absolute certainty once reigned. The belief system seems a bit archaic. That wonderful myth that held all of life together in a meaningful pattern is coming "unglued." New candidates are baffled at customs which seem to have no legitimation except longevity. They even rebel at elements of their formation which make no sense in the world from which they came. Members of the congregation, at different rates of speed, arrive at different conclusions about congregational commitments and a certain disorder occurs in apostolic work. There are still people who believe in the old system but there are others who want to experiment with the new. Polarization appears between the "old" and "young," which are not necessarily a chronological designation. As individuals in the group, at different rates of speed, begin to call various elements of the structure into question the myth itself comes apart. One of the characteristics of myth is that it cannot survive questioning because that which can be questioned is not self-evidently valid. The period of "decline" marks the end of the myth of the stabilized period.

According to Fitz and Cada, after this period of decline comes a period of transition. The congregation must move on. It cannot stay "unglued" indefinitely. For some groups the transition is to extinction. It is well for us to remember that some 50% of the religious orders which have been founded in the course of history have disappeared. The idea that a religious community, once founded, must go on forever, is fallacious. During the period of transition some orders do go out of existence.

Some groups go into what Fitz and Cada call a "diminished existence." This has been the fate of most forms of religious life which, at one period or another, were the paradigmatic form. They continue as a meaningful way of life; they still have some candidates; they still do good work in the Church; but they are not at the very center of developments in religious life.

Finally, there are groups whose transition involves a period of refoundation and revitalization, a kind of corporate renewal. They see the possibility of new life and take steps to bring it about. According to Fitz and Cada such revitalization can take place in three different ways. Sometimes it takes place through a transforming response to the signs of the times. The whole organization is transformed because the societal and ecclesial realities are in such a dramatic state of reformulation that the congregation spontaneously responds in kind. The congregation redefines itself in terms of the new social and ecclesial context.

A second kind of refoundation is the reform that consists in the reappropriation of the founding charism. The Cluniac and Cistercian reforms of the Benedictine monasteries were examples of this kind of transition. The reformers referred to the original Rule of St. Benedict and revived the life of monasticism.

Finally, refoundation and revitalization can be brought about by a profound renewal of the interior life. Teresa of Avila's reform of Carmel was of this type. Teresa's aim was a revitalization of contemplation. She did not go back to Elijah or even to the medieval founder of the Carmelite order. She saw that contemplation was the heart of Carmelite life and that every Carmelite should be a contemplative. This marked a new beginning of the Order.

Which of these three kinds of renewal is most likely to succeed? All of them have to go on together, to some extent, if there is going to be a genuine revitalization. But Fitz and Cada observe that one or another will tend to predominate in any movement of refoundation, according to the period of history in which the revitalization takes place. If the decline happens in a time of massive societal and/or ecclesial change, the emphasis will be on the transforming response to the signs of the time. If the societal and Church situation is fairly stable, the revitalization is more likely to emerge out of interior renewal and express itself as spiritual revival rather than as external change.

It seems to me that the revitalization under way in 20th century religious life began in response to massive societal and ecclesial change. We are probably living through one of the most cataclysmic periods of cultural change in world history. The dawning of world consciousness would not have been possible except for the communications revolution of this century. The liberation movements of our time which are radically modifying human relationships at the personal and collective levels are distinctly 20th century phenomena. Religious life, to be relevant at all, must respond to the massive transformation of society and Church which is the context of our lives today. On the other hand, the very depth of the transformations in which we are involved suggests that, unless the modifications of our life-style and ministerial involvements are accompanied and transfused by a profound interior renewal, the new super-structure will be unable to stand in the crosswinds of the nuclear century.

In summary, we have seen, first, that the relationship between forms of religious life and the social/ecclesial context is deep and determining. This determination is some-thing which we must, on the one hand, appreciate and utilize and, on the other, not allow to neutralize our prophetic witness. Secondly, we have reviewed the pattern of development and decline of religious congregations in the past. Many congregations today are at a point of transition and the choices they make now and in the immediate future will largely determine whether they are oriented toward extinction, diminishment or revitalization.

Lecture III:
Some Implications of the Reflection of History

Having briefly surveyed the history of religious life and highlighted some trends and patterns observable in this history, I would like to discuss six topics which are not intrinsically or logically related to each other but which seem to me to be implications of the historical reflection in which we have been engaged.

I. IMPORTANCE OF OUR ATTITUDES TOWARD HISTORY

I have previously mentioned one implication, namely, the importance of our attitudes toward history. If we are completely unreflective about history, it dominates us. The more reflective we become the more aware we are that we are historical creatures and that history is a process in which we are involved. We can thus relate more creatively to the dimensions of time and change in our life.

Increasing historical awareness helps us to avoid rigidity on the one hand and fatalism on the other. Rigidity is the result of a conviction that because things are a certain way they *have* to be that way. Fatalism results from the conviction that we have no control over the way things develop. It is true that we have no choice about being historical crea-

tures. The idea that we can somehow lift ourselves out of
history by our own boot straps and establish ourselves on
some ahistorical peak from which to watch the train of history in a detached and objective way is part of a world-view
that is incompatible with contemporary science and philosophy. We have no choice about *whether* we will participate
in history but, to some extent, we do have a choice about
how we participate. Notice, I say "to some extent." We do
not have an absolute choice about how we participate in
history. Once certain experiences have taken place, we cannot simply reverse them. About the nuclear arms race,
someone remarked: "One of the truly devastating things
about it is that even if both sides agree to call off the arms
race and get rid of all nuclear weapons, we will always know
that we could build them again if we wanted to." We cannot
return to the innocence of the pre-nuclear age. For the rest of
the history of the human race we will have to deal with
nuclear possibility.

The same is true with regard to experiences in religious
life. The underlying assumptions in a recent document from
Rome, "Essential Elements in the Church's Teaching on
Religious Life as Applied to Institutes Dedicated to Works
of the Apostolate" (1983), is that we have reached the end of
the period of experimentation and that we can now return,
wiser for the experience, to the religious life of the 1950's. It
assumes that life is comparable to an experiment done in a
laboratory in which the experiment does not change the
experimenter. But it is not possible to go back because once
one has had certain experiences they are built into one's
consciousness. We do have a choice about how our experiences will be integrated into our lives. We are not on an
historical freight train that is roaring into the night. We do
not have absolute control over our future but to know something about history is to acquire some kind of control of our
situation.

A second advantage of a more reflective attitude toward
history is an increased ability to use historical resources in
dealing with various issues. Historical resources can help us

to challenge the essentialist approaches. A developed historical consciousness makes us realize that things have been different and will be different again. Our imaginations, in other words, cannot be called off by a definition, no matter how often or by whom that definition is repeated.

We can also learn from the historical process how to exercise patience. Some mistakes, after all, have already been made. Rather than repeating them, we can use our energy creatively. We will no doubt make new mistakes, but hopefully they will be more imaginative than their predecessors. History, in short, is not only baggage from the past; more importantly, it is a resource for the future.

II. UNDERSTANDING OUR LEADERSHIP ROLE AS WOMEN IN THE CHURCH

A second area in which historical understanding might have implications for us today is in our effort to understand and appreciate our leadership role as women in the contemporary Church. It would be helpful for us to go back and study some of the specifically feminine developments in religious life such as the Beguine movement in the Middle Ages. We might also reflect on the numbers, distribution, and historical situation of women religious today. And we might study the feminist movement in the world as a whole. This historical investigation would help us understand how and why we find ourselves corporately in a leadership position today — a strange position for us to be in. Women have not been in such a position in the Church since about the 14th century. History can help us understand why our position is unusual; why it is so threatening to men in the Church; why it might make us have strange and unsettled feelings about ourselves at times. History can assist us in understanding and eventually accepting the role that is historically ours.

Something else we might learn from the history of religious life is that for many reasons we are more likely to find allies among Brothers than among some clerical religious. We need to cultivate that friendship and collaboration.

Furthermore, history can help us to understand why the dialogue between ourselves and certain agencies of the Vatican is so difficult. Understanding does not solve the problem, but at least it helps us realize that the difficulty is not necessarily due to entrenched bad will on their part or proud disobedience on ours. Rather, the historical developments which have influenced us are different in many respects from those which have influenced church authorities. Perhaps some bridges cannot be built. One of the things we can learn from history is that we must come to grips with limits. The notion that everything can be fixed up, that the optimal solution can be arrived at in every case, is an illusion. We all have to learn this for ourselves personally as we go through the mid-life crisis of limits, and as communities we have to learn it corporately. There are certain things that we want to do but are never going to be able to do. That is what it means to be an historical creature, to be a limited, contingent, non-absolute being.

Finally, we can learn from historical reflection that we, as American Catholic religious women, are moving along with other Catholics in this country out of the ghetto and into the mainstream of American life. A significant moment in this process was the election of a Catholic president. Over a period of several decades American Catholics have been involved in this process of "mainstreaming." On the other hand, the movement is going in exactly the opposite direction in Europe. There Catholicism was historically the state religion and virtually everyone was Catholic. Today European Catholics are becoming marginalized and ghettoized. With the cultural dynamics working in opposite directions on the two continents, our experiences are profoundly different from those of European Catholics. What might be terribly important to a Catholic community in Europe which is losing its identity, losing its cultural leverage, becoming marginalized, might be counterproductive in a culture like ours in which the Church is entering the mainstream. An appreciation of cultural relativity is a result of studying history, culture, and sociology.

III. REFLECTIVE RELATIONSHIP TO CULTURE

The third area in which there are implications to be drawn from our historical reflections is our relationship with our own culture. This is an area where it behooves us to be reflective lest we simply drift with the current. Sociologists tell us that too much cognitive dissonance is not healthy. Cognitive dissonance is a lack of harmony between one's way of thinking and that of the group in which one is involved. Too much cognitive dissonance, especially if it is accompanied by behavioral marginalization, leads to ghettoization. Jewish ghettos in the time of the Second World War were a good example of how cognitive dissonance and behavioral marginalization create a private society. As a Church in this country, we do not want to be ghettoized. We have more or less incorporated ourselves into society as an American Church. We want to participate fully in the political, economic and social processes of our society. We want to bring our values as Christians and as Catholics to bear upon these processes.

Too little cognitive dissonance, on the other hand, leads to cooptation. In his book *Do We Need the Church?*, Richard McBrien points out that this second alternative has a built-in escalation factor. In pre-Vatican II days we were almost completely culturally different from our contemporaries. We wore dress that in no way could be confused with secular clothes. We followed the horarium of an agrarian monastery so that we were up when other people were in bed, and in bed when most other people were up. When our life was so cognitively dissonant and behaviorally marginal to the larger culture, it was fairly easy to maintain. We did not feel embarrassed when we went out in our habits or insisted on what we now regard as very strange rules. The whole system hung together as a separate sociological reality. However, as that reality began to break down and there was a greater cultural melding, even slight differences became more difficult to handle. Once we started wearing regular clothes we had to begin to wonder whether they looked like other people's clothes. Dowdiness or unfamiliarity with fashion began to make us nervous. Here we have an example of how the built-in escalation factor functions. The more one melds with the surrounding culture the greater the tendency to be simply absorbed by it.

We need to be able to distinguish between what is really valuable in our culture and what is not. American society is still the carrier of an ideal of democracy and republican government and an ideal of equality that continues to ferment liberation movements. Our basic compassion for the unfortunate of society, our desire for a society in which all can participate, our basic repugnance for violence are all American values. But we need to distinguish between that which is of value and with which we want to cooperate and that which we might simply absorb because it is familiar and easy but which is perhaps not so valuable. One of the reasons for studying history and culture is to make us more able to distinguish between genuine cultural values and societal dross so that we can foster the former and resist the latter.

IV. THE PROBLEM OF CHARISM

A fourth area in which reflection on history and culture might be helpful to us is that of charism, a problem area that has continued to exercise congregations founded in the nineteenth century. A few years ago, many congregations went through endless and largely useless conversations about their distinctive charisms. We finally seemed to have exhausted the topic and, admitting little progress, went on to other things. But the subject of charism keeps reappearing. We wonder whether a certain new ministry is compatible with the charism of our founders. But then we realize that we really do not know what that charism is. The study of history might be helpful on this point for those of us who belong to 19th century foundations.

Most of our founders and foundresses lived in the midst of the post-Tridentine period, the most stable period in the history of the Church. Roman Catholicism had been virtually uniform for hundreds of years in doctrine, morality, liturgy, and daily practice in every country of the world. What founders and foundresses responded to was not a call to reinvent religious life but a call to meet a felt need in society: a need for education, or health care, or social work. They responded to that need by founding a religious congregation to meet it. They were not in the position of a Francis of Assisi coming to realize that enclosed monastic life would not work for his friars and therefore that a new form of religious life had to be founded. Consequently, they did not create something radically new — a new form of life or a new spirituality. Therefore, the search for a kind of radical charism tends to be somewhat futile. One founder's approach does not look very different from the approach of others who founded congregations during this same period.

Does this mean there is no congregational charism? I do not think so. I believe that the great gift to the Church, the charism, is the *fact* of foundation, the fact that somebody was gifted to found an institution and that it worked. Many foundations did not last, but some did, no doubt because the Holy Spirit graced them to continue. It seems to me that this is where we must look for the spirit of the founder.

Perhaps the "spirit" can better be discerned in what has lasted than in what was first proposed. I am suggesting that the search for the spirit of the congregation should be more historical than archaeological. Rather than going back to the beginning of our history to see what was there from the first, our question might be about what has lasted through time. Ours might be a process of looking back from where we are and asking: "What common history have we shared which we can recognize as continuous with our beginnings?" If we start with the foundation and try to discern the distinctiveness in that original adventure, we will find that a certain apostolic work was the original source of unity. This leads to identifying "charism" with "work", a ministerial dead-end in a changing cultural/ecclesial situation.

However, if we look back over history and claim it as shared identity, we will not be mired in a sterile archaism. We may not know how to name it, but there is some reason why we call ourselves IHM's or CSJ's or SND's. When we all break into laughter at some in-group story or remembrance, we are testifying to a shared history, to moments that have become common property, to struggles we have survived together, trivialities we made important and important matters we have trivialized. We are bearing witness to a common memory, a shared present, a future that belongs to all of us. To identify shared history and to claim it we do not have to come up with a theological definition of the charism of an apostolic congregation. Shared history is sufficient for identity.

Finally, I think it is true to say that we do not have the historical perspective necessary to give a definitive answer to the question of charism. Many of our apostolic congregations are not even one hundred and fifty years old. It is one thing to look back to the 13th century, see all the developments of Franciscan life since that period, identify that which held firm for seven centuries, and then conclude from this to the charism of the order. But how can we possibly, from our standpoint in history, get this kind of perspective on a foundation little over a century old? Historical perspective is not something one can generate in response to a command. There has to be a certain distance from the phenomenon in question before one can make these kinds of judgments.

V. THE INTERIORIZATION OF RELIGIOUS VALUES

A fifth area in which historical reflection might be very useful is that of trends in the history of religious life. One such trend has been from the very material realization of values in religious life toward more interiorized realizations. For example, the value of resistance to co-optation by secular culture was originally realized by physical flight to the desert. The same was true of other religious values such as regularity of prayer, poverty, and community life. But we have seen that, in regard to one after the other of these perceived values, they tended, after their initial incorporation in material form, to be somewhat dematerialized in the effort to distinguish the value itself from certain cultural forms. Religious sought other ways to express the value itself so that the rigidity of a single material expression would not tyrannize people, and the value itself might be more flexibly incorporated into religious life. Let us glance briefly at some of the values which have been perceived as important for religious but which are tending to be dematerialized and interiorized in our time as we struggle to understand them more spiritually and live them more deeply and flexibly.

One such value is community life, which has been understood for centuries as "common life." The "common life" definition of community is physical presence together in the same place, at the same time, doing the same things, hopefully animated by an inner spirit. Today we realize that this is an inadequate definition of community life. In fact, common life probably is not essential to community life. Many religious who are excellent communty members are not living the common life. This leads us to seek a less material, more interior understanding of this important value.

What will emerge from this quest? I do not think any of us knows at this point. We are looking for a more flexible understanding of the value we want to affirm when we speak of community life. That value has little to do with physical togetherness but much to do with personal belonging. Dolores Curran has published a book on the traits of a healthy family (Winston, 1983). At the beginning of the book she talks about the way in which the functions of the family have changed in the past few decades. In the 1800's no one would have accepted that divorce could be justified on the grounds of relational inadequacy. If the husband was a good provider, that is, if he went to work every day and brought home his pay check to support the family, he was fulfilling his essential duties as husband and father. If the wife had complained that he showed no affection to her or his children, she would have been told that she basically had a good marriage; the essentials were being provided. And if the wife had the meals on the table, the children clean, and the wash done, her husband had no real right to complain that she was not a loving companion. Today if the relationship is not life-giving, many thinking people consider that grounds for divorce. The function of the family has changed. It is not the husband's function merely to provide, nor the wife's merely to keep house. Today's family is primarily a relational unit rather than an economic one.

I think we are undergoing a similar change in function in religious communities. We are asking questions about whether community life is essentilly a matter of physical presence to one another, or whether it is a matter of psychological and spiritual support and of corporate identity. We can no more be satisfied with common life than marriage partners can be satisfied with economic partnership. Communities, like families, are primarily relational units and we are seeking ways to make this value real in our lives.

Another religious value, poverty, was once defined primarily in terms of financial expenditures. Most of us have feelings of ambivalence in regard to poverty. We want to witness to a simple lifestyle; we want to show some solidarity with the poor. But after a certain amount of experimentation we are beginning to realize that simplicity can easily become conspicuous non-consumption. We are beginning to be sensitive to the fact that chosen imitations of the poor can sometimes be insulting to the poor. We sometimes find we are thrifty in small matters and extravagant in large ones. So we are forced to ask: "What does poverty mean?" It was easy enough to understand poverty when it was practiced in easily specified material ways, such as asking permission for every item of use and holding all things in the convent in common. Today it is impossible for every sister to have exactly the same things as every other. Technological tools, travel, professional wardrobes, continuing education are necessary parts of living ministerial lives. But if poverty is truly a religious value, and the whole history of religious life demonstrates that it is, then we have to find a way to understand poverty which is not totally material and which at the same time, is not completely divorced from material considerations.

A third area in which we are doing the same kind of reflection is that of public witness. The provincial of a community of Brothers recently wrote a theologically sound response to the Vatican document "Essential Elements of Religious Life." When he got to the section which says that while the habit is not the sum total of public witness, it is certain that public witness cannot be given without it, he wrote: "This is patent nonsense." And I think we have to agree. Jesus did not wear a habit and he certainly gave public witness. We are convinced of the value of public witness on the part of persons who have entered an ecclesial state of life. But the question is: "What constitutes public witness?" To say that such witness cannot be given without certain physical signs is historically not true. But if *that* is not true, then what *is*? We are in quest of an understanding of public witness that will be interior, flexible and convincing in our own historical/cultural context.

Obedience is a fourth area for this kind of reflection. Obedience also has been understood in a rather material way: observance of rule and submission to superiors. In times past, we *knew* what it meant to obey because there was strict equivalence between God's will and the material command. Today we are asking how we discern to what God is calling us, individually and corporately. We have to take into account societal demands, personal demands, congregational demands, relational demands. We are not nearly so certain what obedience means or how to practice it but we are certainly very convinced that it is a value central to religious life.

A fifth area that calls for our reflection is consecrated celibacy. Defined materially, celibacy was clear in former times. One was to have no private relationships with anybody of either sex. One of the first things we learned in the postulate was the guiding rule of all communication: "seldom one, Never two, always three or more." The basic point was that we were to have no particular friendships.

Since there is no such thing as a general friendship, this amounted to no friendships at all. Today, we know that relationships are very important to health and maturity. Whether one forms friendships with members of one's own or of the other sex, we are all sexual beings. And so we must find the answer to the question: What does celibacy mean? What does it mean to live in a state of consecrated celibacy when one is involved in deep, intimate, personal relationships, particularly with persons of the opposite sex? Again, the purely material answer — do not touch anyone — will not do. Celibacy must be thought through by today's religious who need an understanding of this value which is less materialistic but no less faithful than the understanding of times past.

Another area that is much debated among religious today is that of perpetual commitment and perseverance once defined in terms of chronological time. It was never, of course, thought that merely staying in the congregation until death exhausted the ideal of perseverance. But the context of commitment was time, from the time one entered until the time one died. The challenge was to work at the quality of the commitment but the parameters of it were defined chronologically. Today, we are asking many questions about the possibility of lifelong commitment for young people, its meaning and its value. The value which perpetual commitment tries to express is fidelity, a value which was well expressed at one point in history by the notion of perseverance through chronological time. Time has something to do with fidelity but the two are neither equivalent nor coextensive. Perhaps there are other measures of fidelity that are even more important than time. In any case, we are again faced with the challenge of how to embody a religious value in flexible, meaningful contemporary expression.

A seventh issue which we are in the process of re-thinking is the very conception of religious life as a state of life. In times past a state of life meant total institutionalization. Some time ago a sociological study was written on prisons, religious life, and the army as three examples of "total institutions." A total institution is one which embraces and regulates every aspect and detail of a person's life. People who live in a prison, even though they do the same kinds of things that people do on the outside, e.g. they exercise, read and watch television, know that their every motion is entirely structured by the fact that they are in prison. Religious life used to be that way. Twenty-four hours a day, fifty-two weeks of the year, one was a religious in every detail of one's life. Religious today are just as totally involved in their commitment but they do not see a need to regulate and institutionalize every detail in order to express that commitment. Minute uniformity and total regulation are not the essence of a state of life.

What then does it mean to say that religious life is a public state of life in the Church? Phenomenologically, a state of life is constituted by a set of stable relationships. For example, marriage is a set of stable relationships to spouse, children, in-laws. No doubt there is much more to a state of life than this, but it would seem that relationships are the constitutive element. Understanding religious life in terms of the relationships it involves is a dematerializing of our approach to this issue.

Membership is another area, another value of religious life, that we are in the process of trying to re-think. Membership, understood univocally, is established by perpetual profession of the three vows. There is a very clean line between members and everybody else. But that boundary is becoming blurred. We are beginning to ask ourselves whether "belonging"might not be a much more inclusive concept. Perhaps we have surrendered some important values and even people to an overly legalistic definition of membership.

There are other values that are undergoing the same kind of re-evaluation but my point here is simply that one of the ways in which historical reflection can be useful for us is by providing us with resources for the re-evaluation in which we are involved. We can inquire into the different ways in which these values were realized in times past and examine some of the ways they were institutionalized or embodied. And this can suggest possibilities and directions for the future.

VI. THE PROBLEM OF DEFINING RELIGIOUS LIFE

Finally, a sixth area which I think it is important for us to reflect on in the light of history is the problem of defining religious life. Many of us had more or less put that topic aside until the appearance of this latest document from the Congregation for Religious on the "Essential Elements of Religious Life," which again raised the question of how to define religious life. We know some approaches that do not work any more. One of them is the comparison approach: that religious life is a higher form of life, a better way of being a Christian, a more intense following of Jesus. Unfortunately, this most recent document abounds with the language of superiority and elitism. But religious themselves rebel against this approach. It not only seems quite contrary to the Gospel but it also does not seem to work. We all know lay people who are just as intense in their Christian commitment as we are, if indeed anyone can measure such a thing! We do not tend to see our lives as a higher form of life. The superiority approach to religious life is bankrupt.

Defining religious life in terms of the evangelical counsels is also very problematic. There is a theological problem with the very notion of evangelical counsels, that is, that there are commands in the Gospel which oblige all Christians and counsels which are intended only for those who choose them. Biblical scholarship has shown that this is not the case. All of the Gospel is intended for all Christians. People in different states of life live the Gospel demands in various ways but no part of the Gospel is the private preserve of religious. Defining religious life as the life of the evangelical counsels is inadequate.

A third approach — that of defining religious life in terms of certain essential elements — is also historically suspect. With the exception of consecrated non-marriage for the sake of the Reign of God, no "element" of religious life has been constant throughout history. Religious life is not a collection of essential elements.

So, how might we go about defining religious life? I think one possible approach that might be worth investigating is the phenomenological approach. I remember once asking a mathematician friend: "What is a mathematician? What is mathematics?" She answered: "Mathematics is new every day. I guess you could say mathematics is what mathematicians do." This definition is a good model for us in our effort to define religious life. Religious life is what real religious do, not what someone imagines as appropriate for theoretical religious. What do real religious do? Many very different things. Religious life is new every day and religious go through a kind of constant, ongoing, corporate discernment process about the appropriateness and significance of the way they are living.

A critically phenomenological approach would validate the experience of people who are sincerely living religious life today, people who are recognized by themselves, by one another, and by other people as religious. It would also allow for the emergence of new experiences of religious life which would not be forbidden at the outset because they did not fit some *a priori* essential definition of this form of life. Such an approach would be less rationalistic and more intuitive, a frightening prospect for people who are more concerned with control than with freedom.

Formation to religious life understood intuitively would rely less on modifying attitudes and behavior and more on the formation of the imagination. Imagination, long considered a suspect and irresponsible faculty of unreality, is being rehabilitated in contemporary study, especially theology. Imagination is our world-constructing capacity. It enlists and unifies intellect, will, and feelings in the creation of a whole which becomes the context within which we can see, interpret, understand and evaluate. Most of us can remember the process of imagination formation in our early training. The directress of formation delivered her most devastating criticism, not when she objected to some particular action but when she said or implied that we lacked the "spirit of the congregation." One did not know what to do to repair the damage because the fault was not in one's actions but in one's very being. Somehow, one was fundamentally out of harmony with what being a member of the congregation was all about. The censure was actually forming our imagination, giving us a *feeling* for what it meant to be part of the congregation.

Forming the imagination is a much more difficult task than teaching someone to behave properly because the formation person has to have an intuitive grasp of religious life, an imagination of religious life, that gives her a feel for the compatibility or lack of compatibility of various ideas, feelings and behaviors with a "world" that is much more than an organization. Perhaps one of the reasons why formation is so difficult today is because the collective imagination is in a state of transition and the world into which new members are being initiated is not stable enough, in the aftermath of the conciliar revolution, to be envisioned clearly.

I am suggesting that a phenomenological approach to understanding religious life which aims at forming the imagination might have more of a future than arguing over "essential elements." Religious life is not a superior form of life, not the life of the evangelical counsels, not a Platonic essence which is realized in a variety of historical incarnations. Rather, it is a movement in the Church which sprang up in response to the preaching of the Gospel. The Church has always had religious and, in my opinion, it always will. But we must realize that a movement is by its very nature fluid. Like a river it flows through various terrains. Sometimes it flows down a mountain and becomes a waterfall. At another time, it is narrowed by its historical terrain and appears to be a mere stream or even sluggish creek. But its source is the fount of revelation and its goal is the ocean of divine love. To turn this flood into a carefully bounded and manageable pond is disastrously to misunderstand the gift of God which is living water springing up unto eternal life.

Conclusion

In these three presentations we have been attempting to mobilize the resources of history for an expanded under-standing of religious life today. In the first presentation we gathered those resources by surveying the history of religious life. In the second we attempted to discern certain trends and patterns that were visible in that long history. And in the final presentation we have tried to bring these historical resources to bear upon some problem areas of contemporary religious life. I hope to have shown that history is definitely on our side. We are living through one of the most difficult and exciting periods in the history of this movement. The shape of our life is undergoing seismic shifts. But religious life is not an essence; it is a movement. And the faculty with which we struggle for understanding of this movement is not the naked intellect but the imagination. We are involved in the historical process of re-imagining, of re-constructing the world that is religious life. We are not the first generation to have faced such a task, but we face it with a much wider array of resources than any previous generation has had at its disposal. This richness is an ambiguous gift because it makes our task much more complex even while it enhances the possibilities of success. Perhaps we can find special encouragement in the realization that we are involved in creating the religious life that the next generation will live. Creation, the work of the imagination, is never easy, but it is, after all, the essential human vocation.

Toward a Theology of the Vows
Juliana Casey, IHM

Although innumerable tomes have appeared on almost every aspect of theology, church, renewal, contemporary significance of ministry, very little has been written on the theology of religious vows. Religious have been too busy trying to live the vows within the context of the enormous changes of the past twenty years to be able to "write the vision down." After two decades of such experience, I suspect that we are now ready to begin — not to finish! — working on a theology of the vows. Our naming of our experience will question us and our lives. Further, such a process will be hope-filled and affirming of ourselves and of the presence of God in our lives.

Language in Scripture

A great deal of research has been done recently on the different kinds and functions of language. This is particularly true of scripture studies. Two of the most significant forms of language in the scriptures are those of parable and myth, which perform two very important functions within the revelation that is God's word. A parable disposes, as one author has said, while a myth proposes.[1] The myth is a story that one tells in order to make sense out of experience, to place experience within a larger context so that one may begin to comprehend its true import. Myths are true when they so function. They are not make-believe stories but are, rather, ways of making sense of life, giving our own lives a larger meaning. A myth grounds our past: how did we come to experience ourselves as sinners, for example. It orients us toward a future: will we eventually be saved? And myth makes some sense of our present: our discomfort; our sense of guilt calls us to conversion, always with the hope that forgiveness is possible. Religious have lived their lives within the context of myth and have found meaning in such a context. For centuries religious life has been viewed in terms of the search for holiness, which leads one away from the temptations of the world and directs one toward a single-hearted striving for perfection through strict observance of the Rules and practices of religious life. That direction, and the myth which grounded it, has given many saints and much grace to the Church. Past decades, however, have made us somewhat uncomfortable with old myths, and the old wineskins do not always hold the new wine very well.

I would like to suggest that we turn to another form of language for enlightenment: the parable. Parables are stories which do not ground meaning so much as disrupt accepted meanings in light of new ones. Parables overturn myth; they shock us. Parables end worlds, not all worlds, but many comfortable ones. For example, part of the myth of religious life held that religious congregations would be started with a small number and, if they were doing the work of God, would prosper, would grow, become more numerous and — very often — establish more institutions. We know that we live now in a time when that myth does not

---

[1]John Dominic Crossan, *The Dark Interval: Towards a Theology of Story*, Niles, Ill.: Argus Communictions, 1975.

hold true to our experience. Religious who proclaim the gospel with their lives, who feed the hungry, who clothe the naked, who give totally of themselves in service to their sisters and brothers *are* doing the work of God. At the same time, religious congregations are smaller in number; religious institutions are closing rather than growing. What does this mean? Are we to say that what we thought was God's work is not? Or, shall we say that the myth no longer applies? Perhaps a parable can help us.

"He said therefore, 'What is the kingdom of God like? And to what shall I compare it? It is like a grain of mustard seed which a man took and sowed in his garden; and it grew and became a tree, and the birds of the air made nests in its branches'" (Lk 13:18-19). For many of us, this parable has traditionally been a comforting promise of growth, of success. Not so for those to whom Jesus originally spoke the parable! Contemporaries of Jesus had treasured traditions about trees and birds who made their nests in such trees. These people would recall the promises of the prophets Ezekiel and Daniel about great and mighty trees: "Behold, I will liken you to a cedar in Lebanon, with fair branches and forest shade, . . . So it towered high above all the trees of the forest; its boughs grew large and its branches long, from abundant water in its shoots. All the birds of the air made their nests in its boughs . . ." (Ezek 31:3-14. Compare: Ezek 17:22-24; Dan 4:10-12). One of the favored images for the coming of God's reign was that of a cedar of Lebanon — a mighty, lofty tree able to provide shelter for all. But Jesus told a parable: the kingdom of heaven is really like a rather insignificant plant. The mustard bush was a wild plant; nobody would cultivate it in a garden. All those who viewed their future in terms of mighty cedars would not be very happy to contemplate God's kingdom in terms of a mustard bush. And yet, Jesus says, that is the way it is in the kingdom . . . and the birds still build their nests.

Parable time is a time that surprises us and forces us to change a lot of our expectations. It is, in a way, a frightening time. It is also the time of the One who speaks to us, Jesus.

We are in a time, I believe, of grace and of unfolding revelation of God. It is important to remember that after one of his parables, Jesus turned to his disciples and said: "To you it has been given to know the secrets of the kingdom of God" (Lk 8:10// Mt 13:11). These words were spoken to people who were neither brilliant, nor great scholars, nor even particularly outstanding. They were very ordinary people. The secrets of the kingdom were in their hearts because they had encountered them in following Jesus. What I hope to do in this article is to look at the parable of what has happened to our experience of living the vows in our world, and to our theological understanding of those vows. I will do so conscious of the fact that we, too, are graced with being friends of Jesus and therefore, even though we are very ordinary people, we have the possibility of the gift of the secrets of the kingdom in our hearts.

I will attempt to offer a brief and very simplified historical overview of the development of religious vows; and to suggest a beginning wording of a theology of the vows as they are lived today and as they point to a future. In so doing, I will take into account three sources for theology. First, the Sacred Scriptures and Tradition of our church. The scriptures are always our testing ground and our guide. Tradition is our history and our roots. Both are integral to our understanding. Second, cultural influences. The world in which we live influences us enormously and has many implications for our understanding of how God would have us be. Third, personal experience. The miracle of the Incarnation tells us that our own human lives are a locus for revelation because God has chosen to become human and to live among us.[2]

---

[2] For further study of the importance of all three sources of theology see: James D. Whitehead, Evelyn Eaton Whitehead, *Method in Ministry: Theological Reflection and Christian Ministry*, New York: The Seabury Press, 1980.

Historical Overview[3]

Perhaps the earliest example of religious vows appears in the book of Numbers. Num 6:1-21 speaks about young men (called Nazirites) who took vows to perform a good work, usually to offer a specific kind of sacrifice to God. When they took these vows, they were consecrated to God for a period of time during which they were forbidden to shave their beards or cut their hair. They were also forbidden to indulge in any wine or strong drink, and they were to have no contact with the dead (such contact would make them unclean). At the end of the specified time, the Nazirites were released from their vows and resumed their normal lives.

Num 30:1-16 provides an example of vows taken by women, and, indirectly, speaks to the self-determination of women in that culture. The text is worth citing. It probably needs no comment.

> Or, when a woman vows a vow to the Lord, and binds herself by a pledge, while within her father'shouse, in her youth, and her father hears of her vow and of her pledge by which she has bound herself, and says nothing to her; then all her vows shall stand, and every pledge by which she has bound herself shall stand. But if her father expresses disapproval to her on the day that he hears of it, no vow of hers, no pledge by which she has bound herself, shall stand; and the Lord will forgive her, because her father opposed her. And if she is married to a husband, while under her vows or any thoughtless utterance of her lips by which she has bound herself, and her husband hears of it, and says nothing to her on the day that he hears; then her vows shall stand, and her pledges by which she has bound herself shall stand. But if, on the day that her husband comes to hear of it, he expresses disap-

---

[3]What follows presumes the excellent historical overview given in S. Schneiders, IHM's article in this same book. See also: P. F. Mulhern, "Vow (Practice and Theology of)," *New Catholic Encyclopedia* (New York: McGraw-Hill, 1967), vol. 14, pp. 756-758.

proval, then he shall make void her vow which was on her, and the thoughtless utterance of her lips, by which she bound herself, and the Lord will forgive her. (Num 30:3-8)

The Acts of the Apostles provides us with two examples which appear to resemble the Nazirite vow. In Acts 18:18, Paul "cut his hair, for he had a vow." Acts 21:23 refers to four young men who "are under a vow." These vows, however, do not serve as the beginnings of what we know as the vows today. Their source lies, rather, in choice for celibacy. Writings of the patristic period make this clear.

Within the first century of the Christian era, Ignatius of Antioch wrote of "those pledged to continence, those virgins who are called widows." Justin Martyr (ca. 165) spoke of groups of virgins. By the third century widows and consecrated virgins were acknowledged groups within the church. There is, however, no indication of official public vows before the third century. In 258 Cyprian considered virginity a permanent state from which one could be dispensed only by the bishop. The fourth and fifth centuries give witness, particularly in Egypt, to groups of monks who lived a common life. In 349 Basil wrote the first "Rule" of religious life. This Rule committed the members to a monastery by a bond of stability. One vowed to follow a "life" — a monastic life according to a particular rule. Benedict (5th century) introduced vows of obedience and of conversion of life in addition to the vow of stability. By the twelfth century, the Hermits of St. Augustine professed poverty, chastity, and obedience. By the thirteenth century, Innocent III spoke of chastity, poverty, and obedience as essential to religious life. One can easily see that vows have a long and varied history within our tradition. Even today, poverty, chastity, and obedience are not the only vows which are professed by all religious.

Within that history a distinction arose between simple vows and solemn vows. Solemn vows were professed in many of the earliest religious orders, particularly the monastic and contemplative ones. The differences between the two types of vows have been debated for centuries. Suarez and the Scotists maintained that the difference between a solemn and a simple vow was purely extrinsic and depended upon the declaration of the church. The Thomists, however, maintained that there was an intrinsic difference: that of giving up the use of something as opposed to giving up the thing itself. One either gives up the use of a patrimony, for example, or gives up the patrimony itself. A further distinction is made in terms of marriage. If one contracts a marriage while one is in simple vows, the marriage is still valid. For those under solemn vows, however, any marriage remains invalid.

The history of these two types of vows again illustrates changes and developments within the formation of religious life. Simple vows predominated in the history of the church until the time of Gratian, around 1140. From then until the sixteenth century, the reverse was true. Only solemn vows were accepted. From the sixteenth century until today, simple vows are much more common. Cultural influences are undoubtedly important in this regard. Events such as the French Revolution and its anti-clerical aftermath made the profession of solemn vows nearly impossible. Thus, simple vows were once again accepted within the church.

A vow, according to the Code of Canon Law, is defined as a "deliberate and free promise made to God concerning a possible and better good which must be fulfilled by reason of the virtue of religion."[4] A vow, made freely, concerns a choice for what is seen as possible and as "better." It is, most importantly, a religious act, one made in faith. A religious act is an act of worship which recognizes God acting in us and in our lives. Such an act responds to God's action in gratitude and in conversion. It is important to recognize that the vows have not been primarily "things to keep," but

---

[4]Canon 1191 *Code of Canon Law: Latin-English Edition*, Trans.prepared under the auspices of the Canon Law Society of America, Washington, D.C.: Canon Law Society of America, 1983.

rather occasions for ongoing worship in gratitude and in conversion. The vows have been seen as gift, as something which develops continuously in our lives, which entails both worship and renewal.

Evangelical Counsels

Any interpretation of the vows in religious life inevitably leads one to a discussion of the meaning of the evangelical counsels, for the vows have long been identified with these counsels. The Catholic Encylopedia defines them as: "The advisory directives of Christ, as distinct from the moral precepts, given as guides to closer approximation to perfection and imitation of Christ himself."[5] Many questions have arisen recently concerning evangelical counsels. These questions center around the distinction between "directives" and "moral precepts", particularly as they have been interpreted from scripture, and around the meaning of perfection.

Contemporary scholarship underscores the unity of the gospel message even as it celebrates the diversity of authorship and forms of expression. When the gospel of Jesus Christ is seen as a whole, as the good news of one who has come among us to save us and to invite us to discipleship, it becomes very difficult to say that certain texts are meant for everyone, while others are only for those who want to go beyond the 'minimum.' Jesus' words and ministry show us that there is no "minimum"; there is either acceptance or rejection of God's saving mercy. God's reign transforms all of life and all lives.

Many of the "classic" texts which have served as a basis for the evangelical counsels take on different nuances when examined in the light of modern exegesis. 1 Corinthians 7, for example, has frequently been viewed as a grounding for the higher calling of celibacy. This text, however, must be

[5]J. D. Geken, "Counsels, Evangelical," *New Catholic Encyclopedia*, vol. 4, p. 383.

seen within its own context of an urgent eschatological exhortation. Paul worries not so much about which state of life is better; but about the total dedication of all in a time when, as he views it, the Parousia is imminent. These "classic" texts will be examined in more detail in the sections of this essay which deal with the individual vows.

The meaning of Christian perfection has developed in new, somewhat surprising ways in recent decades. These developments force us to question a structured concept of Christian perfection. A "private" perfection which stressed one's individual relationship to God and which over-stressed the need for removal from the evil world, led to elaborate studies and descriptions of stages and of levels of perfection. R. Garrigou-Lagrange, O.P., in his seminal work, *The Three Ages of the Interior Life*,[6] speaks about the relationship between perfection and the evangelical counsels. His work illustrates the perceived connection between practice of the evangelical counsels of poverty, chastity, and obedience and the attainment of perfection.

> The effective practice of the three evangelical counsels is not obligatory nor is it indispensable to reach the perfection toward which we must all tend, but it is a most suitable means more surely and rapidly to reach the end and not to run the danger of stopping halfway. We have said that a soul cannot reach perfection without having the spirit of the counsels, or the spirit of detachment. Now, it is difficult truly to have this spirit without the effective practice of this detachment, which seemed too hard to the rich young man. Sanctity can be attained in the married state, as we see from the lives of St. Clotilde, St. Louis, and Blessed Anna Maria Taigi, but it is more difficult and more rare to reach it by this common road. It is not easy to have the spirit of detachment in regard to worldly goods, permitted pleasures, and our own will, if,

[6]R. Garrigou-Lagrange, O.P., *The Three Ages of the Interior Life*, trans. by Sr. M. Timothea Doyle, O.P., St. Louis: B. Herder Book Co., 1947.

in reality, we do not effectively detach ourselves from them. The Christian who lives in the world is often exposed to excessive absorption and preoccupations about a situation to be acquired or maintained for himself and his family. (I, p. 207)

The point which Garrigou-Lagrange makes is that practice of the evangelical counsels in religious life is a surer way to reach perfection. Garrigou-Lagrange would agree with the teaching of Vatican II that all are called to holiness, but one surmises that his emphasis would differ from that of the post-Vatican II church. All are called to the same holiness, we are told, and no way of attaining that holiness is more sure, more perfect than another. We are all called to know and to love God. While no one is called to that any more or any less than anyone else, each is called in a unique and specific way. One of the ways is that of vowed religious life. A valid, valuable, wonderful way — but not a more perfect way.

The renewal of religious life in the past two decades has left us with many questions, some myths which don't "fit" any more, worlds which have ended, new worlds which have begun. Most profoundly, this renewal has led many, many religious to new visions, new hopes for their lives. As Vatican II moved the focus of ecclesiology from one directed to a structured institution to that of a people called by God, so too it led religious to a new focus. Previous to the Council, religious life's emphasis was upon perfection, sanctification of the members. This is not to say that religious life had no meaning in/for the world, or that religious themselves were not given to the service and sanctification of others. It is to say, however, that the emphasis, the focus of attention was often directed inward; the important life was the interior life. The transformations of the past twenty years, especially in apostolic religious communities, especially in the United States, have been characterized by a new self-understanding. Religious have begun to understand themselves and their mission in terms of relationship to a world deeply in need of transformation, rather than of flight from a world lost to sin.

The Decree on Religious Life said: "Communities should promote among their members a suitable awareness of contemporary human conditions and of the needs of the church. For if their members can combine the burning zeal of the apostle with wise judgments made in the light of faith concerning the circumstances of the modern world, they will be able to come to the aid of the people more effectively."[7] All religious communities have done this, and it has changed them. The vows, within this context take on new meanings. They are not so much means of perfection as they are vehicles for mission. In other words, our question is no longer how can living poverty, obedience, and celibacy make us perfect. It is, rather, how can we, living poverty, obedience, and celibacy together, transform the world?

It is with the latter question that we turn now to the vows themselves.

[7]Decree on the Appropriate Renewal of Religious Life, #2. In: Walter M. Abbott, S.J., ed., *The Documents of Vatican II*, New York: The American Press, 1966.

Poverty and the Poor

While it is undoubtedly true that one does not live "vows," but rather a "vowed life," it is nonetheless important for us to spend some time examining each of the vows in themselves in order to come to a clearer understanding of how poverty, chastity and obedience each contributes to a meaningful life lived for the sake of the Gospel. In the following pages, each vow will be studied within the larger context of the movement from understanding religious life primarily in terms of a search for perfection, to viewing such a life as it contributes to the transformation of the world and to the unveiling of God's kingdom among us. In each case, three loci of theology will be consulted: Sacred Scripture and Tradition, Cultural Influences, Personal Experience.

If we look at the vow of poverty within the context of removal from the world and a search for individual perfection or sanctification, I think we can say that poverty was seen primarily as renunciation. Some of the ways we expressed that were in the renouncement of any personal ownership, the reception of everything from a superior, the necessity of permission for anything new. One received no gifts that were for personal use; one had no choice concerning personal appearance. One of the major external expressions of Sisters' vows of poverty was their sameness. Everyone looked alike, had the same habits, did the same things at the same time. Ours was a poverty of having nothing, of receiving everything. There is much of value in such an understanding, and in voluntary dependency, particularly if one seeks to renounce the world rather than transform it. For most religious, poverty was a goal toward which we strove with great dedication.

Cultural Influences

If, however, we place poverty within the context of our times, and if we look at what culture and what Scripture and our own experience have to say to us about it, I think we see some different aspects. Whereas poverty was seen primarily as a primitive goal within religious life, in culture, poverty is viewed as a decidedly negative reality. In our culture it is all too often connected with evil, with crime, with dope, or with laziness. It is related to somebody who "doesn't want to work," or to the stereotypical image of the welfare mother who does not take care of her children, and who buys pop and potato chips with her food-stamp money. I recently heard the New York State Commissioner of Human Rights point out that 50% of the black people in our country are below the poverty line. Of this 50%, 7 out of 10 households are headed by single mothers. Poverty is profoundly linked with racism and with sexism. The poor are not merely poor; they are also victims of racial and sexual stereotyping.

Our culture also helps to perpetuate a vicious cycle of poverty. One generation grows up in destitution and continues it into another generation, and there is no way out. All of us remember the comments that we heard a few years ago when companies were involved in equal opportunity and affirmative action programs. "But *they* don't know how to get here on time. They don't know how to punch in at the time clock. They don't want to work." The continuation of a vicious cycle. The drastic increase of poverty among what we have formerly called the "middle class worker" is introducing a new cycle, one which intensifies in despair, feelings of inadequacy, feelings of worthlessness as each day passes. Statistics tell us that employment is rising, but that it is doing so within the area of service jobs. How do unskilled laborers become equipped for this type of employment?

The fact that poverty is viewed as something which is somehow immoral within our culture traces its roots to the very beginnings of our country. Religious men and women are not the only people who have lived within myth. All peoples do. All groups have myths which ground their past, give meaning to their present and orientation to their future. The United States is no exception. Robert Benne and Philip Hefner have studied the myth of America in their work, *Defining America: A Christian Critique of the American Dream* (Philadelphia: Fortress Press, 1974). Benne and Hefner demonstrate that the American myth emerged within a religious context, particularly that of the people of God reaching the promised land. The paradigms for self-understanding in the early American myth were Abraham and Moses. Their stories were the American story. I cite their description:

> In both the Abrahamic and the Mosaic stories, the heroes are elected by God, not because of any particular merit of their own, but because of God's own goodness. And by God's own promises, they are led out of the ordered and predictable world of the past, a past that either was or would become oppressive were the hero not to heed the call. Both characters trust in the promise — both Abraham and Moses. In trust they move from the past, out into the wilderness in which a struggle for new identity takes place. In the midst of harassment, confusion and difficult conditions, a struggling ascent toward the promised land ensues. Accompanying trust in the promise of God is obedience to the law of the Covenant. The promise, and continued trust in it, is contingent upon living up to the demands of God. God's demands rule the internal life of the covenant people. Finally, the promised future is fulfilled. The land flowing with milk and honey is

reached. And lands and sons, the contents of the original promise to Abraham, are realized. Through this covenant of trust and obedience, Israel becomes a light to the nations. Her destiny is to bring new hope to humankind through her faith in the promise. Thus, there is a movement out of the ordered or mastered world of the past into a wilderness struggle for a fuller identity in the present and finally the reaching of God's promises in the gracious future. In this movement, begun by a graceful election and fulfilled in a gracious future, Israel, by her trust and obedience, becomes a paradigm — a beacon — for all peoples and nations." (p. 3)

We all know that story. It is our story as members of God's people. But what happens to that myth when it is adopted — and adapted — by a nation newly born? Benne and Hefner point out that the image of the New Israel appears frequently in early American literature and political rhetoric. For example, when the search for an official seal for the United States took place, Benjamin Franklin proposed a seal in which Moses was lifting up his rod and dividing the Red Sea while Pharaoh was overwhelmed by the waters. The motto was to be: "Rebellion to tyrants is obedience to God." Jefferson proposed one with the children of Israel in the wilderness led by a cloud by day and a pillar of fire by night (p. 4). Neither suggestion was accepted, but the myth persisted and became ". . . clothed in American garb. And the Abraham of Genesis became the Abraham of Illinois" (*ibid.*).

When so clothed, the American myth consisted of three basic steps. First, to leave the past behind — to shake free of a limiting past. Second, to move forward in a struggling ascent. The emphasis here becomes one of climbing, of moving *upward*. Third, to reach the realization of an open and gracious future. Within this myth, to be poor is to have failed the American dream. It is not just unfortunate; it is somehow immoral.

The authors say that there is a dark side to this myth, a side largely ignored until the decade of the 1960's. The fact is that not everyone in the United States left behind a limiting past. Some left behind a very good life. They did not come to an open and gracious future; they came to slavery. Not everyone in this country can climb the ascent, make it to the top of the ladder. When ladders are climbed, there's only a certain amount of room. Most people are pushed off the ladder, or left standing at its foot. It is within this cultural context that religious find themselves called to vow poverty.

Sacred Scripture and Tradition

What have Scripture and Tradition to say to us about poverty? The first place we look is to the Beatitudes and their promise of blessing for the poor. The Beatitudes are Jesus' prophetic announcement of the reign of God. It is important to remember that they are prophetic words, that is, they *do* what they *say*. Jesus cries out in the very first one: "Blessed are you poor, for yours is the kingdom of God"(Lk 6:20/ Mt 5:3). The linguistic background to the terms used in the Beatitudes shows that those spoken of are the poor, those whose very spirit is poor. They are not ones who are "as if" poor. All of Scripture shows us that it is to those in dire need and great longing that God goes.

The Beatitudes, spoken by Jesus and enfleshed by him in his whole life and ministry, are signs of reversal. They disrupt some worlds, while allowing others to enter. The reign of God turns things upside down. It is a mustard bush, not a mighty cedar that becomes symbol of such a reign. The categories of "important" and "valuable" are reversed. These are no longer the ones who have successfully made a "struggling ascent." They are, rather, the ones around the bottom of the ladder. Jesus' proclamation indicates where true blessing is to be found.It is not in success, but rather in the need and vulnerability, and openness to God's reign, which allows God's grace to enter into our lives.

The most undeserving are called to enter the kingdom. We have all become more aware in recent years of the poverty of our own human existence. We are more conscious, often painfully conscious, of our own inadequacies, our own imperfection. This consciousness, I believe, enables us to go a small step further in truly hearing the Beatitudes. In our own need as a people, we discover the call and the belongingness of the kingdom. In our insufficiencies, imperfection, we hear — directed to us "Blessed are *you* poor." In hearing such a message (little wonder the Gospel is Good News!), we find ourselves enabled and impelled to reject the prevalent cultural understanding of the poor. The poor are not immoral, they're not un-American. Theirs is the kingdom. We know ourselves called to value the poor, to reverence their closeness to the One who loves them. We begin to learn to find ways to hear them, to learn from them, to hear the Gospel in their voices. When we, in our own poverty, know the gift of God's reign in our lives, we find ourselves struggling alongside the poor for the full realization of the kingdom of God. Perhaps a vow of poverty is a promise to indeed reject what our culture says about the poor. It is also to refuse to place anyone's value (our own included) in wealth, security, status, role. The most valuable, says the Gospel, are the most needy.

One of the classic texts historically used to interpret the vow of poverty is that of the rich young man in Matthew 19:16-22 (// Lk 18:18-30; Mk 10:17-31). The text describes an encounter between Jesus and a young man who asks "What must I do to have eternal life" (Mt 19:16). When Jesus responds that the young man must keep the commandments, the questioner replies that he does so. Jesus then says to him, "If you would be perfect, go, sell what you possess and give to the poor, and you will have treasure in heaven; and come follow me." (19:21) The young man, we are told, went away sorrowful, "for he had great possessions." The Matthean text continues with Jesus' saying that it is easier for a camel to go through the eye of a needle than for a rich man to enter the kingdom of God (v. 24).

This text is important for two main reasons. In the first

place it relates that "perfection" to possession of riches. Perfection in a scriptural context is a complex notion. The term can mean maturity, completion, fulfillment. It rarely has anything to do with following laws or — even — going beyond the laws. In the New Testament, perfection is always related to God's Kingdom, or to the representative of that kingdom — Jesus. When Jesus tells the young man about "being perfect", he calls him to discipleship. Jesus does not answer the question with a lesson in ways of being even "better" than all those who keep the commandments. He answers in terms of choosing the one thing which is necessary — the following of Jesus.

If the young man (or anyone) would be perfect, that is, brought to fulness and completion, he must get rid of everything and follow Jesus. The point of the story is the call to follow Jesus. But the young man is possessed by his riches. We have here the struggle between keeping the rules and thinking that is going to earn eternal life for us, or throwing it all away in order to follow a fellow down the road. The call is to follow Jesus, and the way is liberating oneself from whatever hinders that following; it is to sell everything and to free oneself for discipleship. The priority, Jesus tells us, is God's kingdom. And Jesus is the presence of God's kingdom among us. This call is directed to all, not merely to the few who "already keep the commandments." There is truly sorrow in this story, for the young man did not merely lose "perfection"; he lost everything. He remained possessed by things. Jesus went on down the road.

A more contemporary form of tradition, that of questions posed by present members of the community of faith, presents us with a new call to understand the significance of the vow of poverty. In the 1981 study paper issued by the Latin American Confederation of Religious (CLAR) entitled "The Mission of Religious Life in the Local Church of Latin America," serious questions are posed for all religious who take a vow of povery. The basic question is, "Does our vow of poverty prevent us from being really poor today?" Their reasons for this question are four-fold, and point out with startling clarity the major change which has taken place between a pre-Vatican II enfleshment of the vow, and our post-Vatican II struggles towards reinterpretation.

Their first reason: "We have the possibility of living a kind and level of life that is more rich than poor" points out that while religious communities experience sharing of goods, they usually do so within the communities "but not with the poor." Communities, which began poor, gradually accumulate some measure of security through gifts, contributions, endowments. The individual may give up the riches of the world, but often these riches "follow us, penetrate our institutions, do not give *us* up." The vow of poverty, then, has important — and difficult —corporate ramifications. One can be very "poor", and still live very well.

Secondly, "We do not have to struggle for survival." A religious vocation is often also a profession. One receives support and sustenance from performing religious service. "It is not usual, nor is it normally possible for a religious to be a laborer nor a laborer to be a religious." CLAR is not suggesting that religious do not labor, but rather pointing to the fact that our labor most often differs radically from that of the poor of the world. Because of this, they say, "The vow of poverty prevents us from having contact with material reality through work," (their third reason). Such lack of contact can lead to a 'spiritualization' of poverty. All of us know only too well how easy it is to talk *about* poverty, rather than to actually experience it. Finally, "The vow of poverty makes social and political solidarity with workers and peasants difficult for us." Because we are so often at one-step removed from the actual, physical, debilitating poverty of our brothers and sisters, it is difficult for us to see with their eyes, to ache with their hearts. Consequently, religious often perform for the poor the services that *religious* deem necessary. True solidarity leads to "communion and participation," says CLAR, and "entrusts to the poor the role of deciding what kind of service is needed."

Our sister and brother religious in Latin American pose great challenges to us. We have begun to feel the reality of their questions within our own North American context, and to recognize that our discomfort with our comfort is a gospel call. The CLAR study paper reminds us that a vow of poverty is not merely renouncing personal ownership. It is rather a corporate reality, which involves the communal existence of religious congregations. Poverty, further, must be viewed from within the perspective of the poor of our world. Jesus calls us to follow him, and he inevitably leads us to the poor.

Personal Experience

What can our personal experience contribute to an enriched understanding of the vow of poverty? Religious communities have had some financial difficulties in the past years. In many cases that has made it necessary for religous — who are vowed to poverty — to request higher stipends for their service. Many religious have faced the ambiguity of asking for "more money." And too many have had to listen to employers tell them that they were "not worth it," that religious are "pricing themselves out of business," that we obviously won't be able to work with the poor anymore. These painful experiences have enabled us to know — concretely — what it means to be devalued. We have a sensitivity now that we might never have gained in any other way.

Further, financial difficulties and decreased numbers have forced us to recognize an uncertainty about our future. Not all of us will go on forever. This uncertainty places us in solidarity with the vast majority of our world; and it calls us closer to God's kingdom, where the loving, merciful, ever-present God is the only security. At the same time, our personal experiences in ministry have made us uneasy in face of the cry of the poor. We hear ourselves called to a new awareness of the Gospel blessing of the poor, and a new awareness of the continual call to conversion inherent in living a vowed life.

We have also begun to discover the poverty of our own humanness and the salvation therein. Part of that discovery results from the disappearance of many of the outward signs of poverty in our lives. The external signs such as sameness of dress, permissions from superiors, disassociation from monetary concerns, provided us with objective criteria which often served as "proof" that one was a good religious. The criteria have become more internal, less measurable in our times. Our poverty begins within our own hearts, and in the choices that we make. It is expressed in the ways in which we live, and how we are with each other and with all of our sisters and brothers.

The disappearance of external, universal, objectifiable "signs" of religious poverty introduces us to true Gospel poverty. When one recognizes one's own poorness, one also is led to own one's insecurity. Deep within the discomfort of insecurity, lies the grace-filled call to place oneself within the love and the mercy of an ever-present God. One learns to trust in that God rather than in any external symbols. The enfleshment of that trust in our lives becomes, in turn, a new form of sign, one which promises the riches of the kingdom. The unhappy rich young man becomes the happy poor person who does not need possessions, who is free for discipleship, who can follow a poor Messiah.

The experience of insecurity and the call to trust therein enables us to "let go," both corporately and individually. Congregations have clearly felt insecure in these past years. They are smaller, resembling more a mustard bush than a mighty cedar. They are also getting older. These facts mean that religious communities can no longer do all the wonderful and worthy things they would do. They cannot continue to staff all the institutions they would like, nor to begin the new ministries so urgently needed for our world. This corporate experience of our limits enables us to ask: "Where would God have us be; how would God have us serve in our limited, poor ways?" These questions are gospel questions; they are grace.

Personally letting go empowers us for discipleship because it enables us to let go of cherished presuppositions about where we will be in twenty years, about what we need to survive, what we need to own, to have. We are then freed to discover what we *truly* need. And we are given voices to sing a Magnificat in the midst of our poverty.

Celibacy, Sexuality, and the Single Life

Within the context of vowed life seen as separation from the world in pursuit of sanctification and perfection, the vow of celibacy was expressed in the renunciation of family, spouse, sexual attachments. All too often, this renunciation also implied a woeful lack of adequate information and celebration of one's own sexuality. In giving up "sex," one also gave up "sexuality." Vowed religious were very careful about developing personal friendships or strong emotional attachments. Sometimes this resulted in signs of emotional immaturity, a childishness not consonant with an adult person, or a brusqueness which provided a shell of protection from the temptations of "the flesh."

Celibacy, further, was expressed with a very strong emphasis on modesty. In some instances this stress had valuable "by-products." Thus, "modesty of the eyes" enabled many to provide a privacy for each other, which would otherwise have been impossible in the close living quarters of so many religious houses. At the same time, an overaccentuation on modesty led many of us to devalue that which is integral to who we are — our own bodies.

Excessive modesty, combined with emotional immaturity, subtly affected religious' relationships with members of the opposite sex. Many women religious' relationships with men were in terms of persons who had authority over them. Many women left their father's house, entered a religious motherhouse where, in fact, it was still father who affirmed or denied their goodness. In some cases, the local bishop was the ultimate superior of the community; in others the confessors held great sway. In many monastic communities, the male counterpart of the congregation, made all the decisions. Ultimately, the Fathers of the Sacred Congregation for Religious and Secular Institutes determined the validity of a congregation's life. Religious rules often expressed this. One such rule stated: "The Sisters should be animated by a lively faith in the sacred character of the priesthood, always manifesting a profound reverence for ecclesiastics and in their dealings with them avoid all levity and familiarity. . . ." To be reverent toward others is always necessary, but excessive reverence led many to unexpressed denials of their own feminine value.

The image of the Bride of Christ has often been used to express the meaning of vowed celibacy. This image is one of the richest and most beautiful within our Christian tradition. It is, however, important to remember that it is a mystical concept, used by women such as Teresa of Avila or Julian of Norwich in order to express the profound contemplative union which they shared with the divine. Sometimes, because the image was so widely used, it led to an unhealthy spirituality, where being a Bride of Christ was seen as a substitution for being a bride of Thomas Jones. This is not what Teresa or Julian meant. They were talking about mystical oneness of being.

The church has viewed herself as the Bride of Christ in terms of her ideal purity, union with the Lord, and total devotion. Within this context, vowed celibate life has served as an expression of that total devotion. This is an important gift, which religious life has given the church, and the image of Bride carries great richness within this context. When, however, the image is interpreted in an individualistic, "Jesus-and-me" sense, it is robbed of its meaning.

Cultural Influences

Historically, cultures have often manifested an ambiguity about vowed celibacy. Convents have been seen as places to send the unmarriageable daughter or the incorrigible young woman. They have also been viewed as places where a special holiness dwelt. When sexuality itself is seen as less than holy, and sexual relations are viewed as a necessary evil, those who choose to refrain are somehow holier, more perfect. Religious have served as reminders of another way of living, another possibility of meaning in life. As such reminders, celibate religious have been positive influences in a world which often forgets the all-encompassing call of the gospel.

The most significant cultural influence upon a contemporary understanding of vowed celibacy is that of the women's movement. This movement, which profoundly affects the image, meaning, way of living for the majority of the world's population, has great ramifications in understanding and valuing celibacy. Until recently, young girls expected to grow up, get married, and have children *or* some few chose to enter religious ife. An unmarried woman was either a "nun," or a rather unfortunate spinster. The women's movement has changed that. Today there is a much more positive understanding of the single woman in our culture. It is more acceptable for a woman to delay marriage and/or children for a certain period of time in order to develop her own potential, to use her own gifts. Further, the image of woman as exclusively a child-bearer is very seriously questioned in our culture. Women, by and large, no longer live only for or through their husbands. They are no longer the "little woman." The choice of the single state is a new phenomenon in our culture, one which subtly questions given notions about celibacy. It does so because it implies that there are many reasons for choosing celibacy. What, then, does vowed celibacy in a religious context mean? What does it have to offer to the present culture?

Another influence of the changing roles of women in our time is that of bonding and of networking which takes place throughout the world. Such bonding changes our perspectives about the future for women and about the possibilities for strong, life-giving community outside the confines of religious congregations. Young women today have a much greater range of choices ahead of them. These facts were brought home to me very clearly on a recent train trip. Seated behind me was a young man with his daughter. She was about six years old. Her father was very gentle with her and obviously enjoyed his role as parent. Across the aisle from him were two women (approximately 55-60) who were on their way to a convention of their union. These women began talking to the little girl. At one point, however, the little girl discovered a little boy about four seats ahead of us. They began to play together. The little girl became rather aggressive at one point and the father said, "No, no, you mustn't do that." The father then went on to explain to the child that that wasn't what little *girls* did. That was what little *boys* did. If she continued to act in this way, she would have problems when she grew up. One of the women bristled, turned to the young man and said, "Young man, by the time your daughter is your age, women will be running the world!" Certainly a different vision!

Women have been enabled to view themselves and their meaning in ways other than their relationships to men. The single woman is a growing reality. Statistics show that one-fourth of the population in the U.S. lives alone, and that the numbers are growing. This phenomenon, while it expands possibilities of meaning for both men and women, also causes serious difficulties, particularly in terms of isolation and alienation. The novel (and more recently the film), "Looking for Mr. Goodbar," portrays such isolation in a graphic and tragic way. A dedicated teacher who does marvelous work with handicapped children, the heroine, nevertheless spends her evenings in singles' bars, looking for some means of communicating, some way of relating with others. Her search costs her her life.

Culture has mixed messages about celibacy today. On the one hand, religious women are not the only respected unmarried women. On the other, married women are not significant only because of their husbands. Vowed celibacy takes on new significance in this context.

Scripture and Tradition

What do our tradition and our Scriptures have to say about religious celibacy? First, it is important to re-discover what Scripture does *not* say. One of the most influential texts in terms of celibacy is that of 1 Cor 7:1-9. This text ends with the famous verse: "But if they cannot exercise self-control, they should marry. For it is better to marry than to be aflame with passion" (RSV translation). For centuries this text has been the focus of arguments that celibate life was holier, more perfect than marriage. Contemporary exegetical consensus has concluded that Paul is writing in an eschatological mode here. In other words, the focus of his discussion is preparedness for the return of the Lord. He is talking about being totally prepared, about giving all of one's energies to the waiting. He is not discussing the relative merits of celibacy and marriage.

Another classic text is that of Matthew 19:1-12 concerning "eunuchs who have made themselves eunuchs for the sake of the kingdom of heaven." Again here it would seem that we have a text, a saying of Jesus in this case, which indicates that celibacy for the sake of the kingdom is of higher virtue than the married state: "Not all can receive this saying, but only those to whom it is given" (v. 11). This text, it must be remembered, is within a context of questions about divorce. It does not deal with celibacy *per se*, but rather with divorce and remarriage. "Eunuchs who have made themselves eunuchs for the sake of the kingdom" are those persons who have chosen not to remarry. They are not persons who have decided to enter vowed religious life.

Much discussion has been given to the images of virgins in the Book of Revelation. The point of the image in Revelation is not that virgins will have "higher" places in heaven, but rather that everyone will be a virgin. In the fullness of time all persons will be whole, entire, complete. The virgins are an eschatological image of the final day. Virginity, vowed celibacy, has such an eschatological meaning when it does point to the promised wholeness of the kingdom.

Within the Judaeo-Christian tradition, celibacy has been seen as a negative at times. In Judaism, the command to multiply and fill the earth was taken with great seriousness. It was part of the obligation of the people of God. It was also, it must be remembered, a cultural necessity for a small, minority population whose means of existence depended upon the children who would soon join the labor force. The pervasiveness of this command still influences us today. Moral theologians would do well to examine seriously the influence of this law upon the formulation of sexual morality throughout the centuries.

Barren women are highly symbolic in Hebrew Scriptures and in the New Testament. Births of great heroes most often came as miraculous deliverance of barren women. The great prayers of thanksgiving spoken by these women give witness to the importance of bearing a child. God transformed, delivered those who were barren, who could have been legally divorced by their husbands for their barrenness. Thus, Sarah, barren until her old age, cries out at the birth of Isaac: "God has made laughter for me" (Gen 21:6). And Elizabeth, pregnant with John, prays: "And blessed is she who believed that there would be a fulfillment of what was spoken to her from the Lord" (Lk 1:45). Within this culture, a woman who remained celibate was hardly viewed as entering a higher state.

At the same time, particularly in the early Christian communities, widows had a significant role. They performed important functions within the community and were viewed as having specific ministries. They are probably the origins of religious "orders" (see Sandra Schneiders' article for a fuller explication of the role of widows in the early churches.) Within three to four hundred years, celibacy was seen as a great virtue and as a higher state. This understanding of celibacy must be related to an extremely negative view of sexuality, which predominated during these centuries. Women celibates were especially encouraged, for women were the enfleshment of sexuality and of temptation. For them, to choose celibacy was to deny the tendency to evil that was part of their very make-up as women. Celibate women became something other, something "higher." A quote from St. Jerome illustrates this: "As long as a woman is for birth and children, she is different from man as body is from soul. But when she wishes to serve Christ more than the world, then she will cease to be a woman, and will be called man."[1] Few women would choose celibacy for that reason today!

Tradition also provides us with very positive images of vowed celibacy and the meaning which it speaks. Religious congregations have long been places/spaces where women were able to develop their gifts, to use their skills in ways that would have been unthinkable anywhere else. Research is beginning to reclaim the great celibate women of our history, those whose learning, ministering, building, administrative skills, writing gifts, profoundly influenced and transformed their cultures.

Scripture, too, has much that is positive to say to vowed celibacy. Most importantly, the gospels call—over and over again — to total givenness to the reign of God. Chosen celibacy is an enfleshment of the absoluteness of the demands of the kingdom of God. Celibacy is the "leaving all things" which includes even that which is most instinctive in us — our deepest desires to intimate, healthy, sexual relationships, the continuation of ourselves in our children. To choose celibacy for the sake of the kingdom is to say with one's life that God and God's call take precedence over family, over social structures, over all. To become a happy, whole person in that celibacy is sign to a death-ridden world that God does indeed give life, that following the demands of the kingdom does not diminish but rather enhances one's humanity.

Further, vowed celibacy for the sake of the kingdom is truly an eschatological sign. It is a sign of what all persons will be — whole and fully alive in God. But celibacy is such a

---

[1]Cited by Mary Gordon in "Coming to Terms with Mary," *Commonweal* 109(January 15, 1982) 11-14, p. 12.

sign only when it makes manifest now what is hoped for in the future. Eschatological signs are meaningful because they point not only to the final fullness, but because they also reveal what has already begun in Jesus Christ. Celibacy, then, reveals the freedom, the reconciliation, the communion of the kingdom. Celibacy, chosen in community, becomes an eschatological sign, not merely because it is celibacy, but because it frees persons to be reconciled, to be in communion with each other, to be good news among the poor.

Personal Experience

Our personal, lived experience of celibacy in these our times suggests positive directions for vowed celibacy and important contributions such a life can offer our world. I would like to stress three of those directions. In the first place, we have begun to rediscover the great value of celibacy in community. Once again we hear the gospel call to love one another, and we seek to improve the quality of our lives lived together. Celibacy in community is a positive model of bonding and of women supporting each other. Sometimes I think religious women take that for granted or lose sight of it within the nitty-gritty of daily life. Religious communities have a way of bonding, of counting upon each other for support that is a valuable gift to offer our sisters who do not have such groups.

Recent studies on the psychology and moral maturity of women have pointed out that women grow and mature in terms of relationships. What can celibate communities offer to our sisters in terms of networking, of bonding? The last twenty years have taught a great deal of the "hows" of relating to each other. Can not this experience and a willingness, a welcoming stance be gift and comfort to women who find themselves alone and isolated? Further, more and more women in our culture are refusing to be viewed merely in terms of their sexuality — they will not be sex objects.

What does it mean, what can it say, when hundreds of women, healthy whole persons are celibate by choice? Can that not be an important statement that women are not simply sex objects?

One of the great crises of our times is the plight of the elderly, particularly elderly women. Celibate communities have learned to care for their aged, their sick, their disabled in loving and creative ways. I am convinced that sociologists and gerontologists should study religious motherhouses. Religious are not perfect in their caring, but they have learned a great deal about humane, life-giving care for those who need it. Our experience is a gift to be given to others. Religious have begun to ask questions such as: "What does it mean to be lonely; where is grace in our loneliness?" Perhaps our search will empower others, who are sometimes paralyzed in their aloneness. Celibate persons in community have gold mines of experience and of information with which they can serve their brothers and sisters because they have had to struggle with the same questions, the same problems.

Secondly, celibacy has much to say about freedom for mission. In the first place, vowed celibates are enabled to move, to respond to the needs of God's people with a facility not possible for most people. It is often vowed celibates who are free to be healing presence in the aching spots of our world. Celibacy in community also allows for the training and re-training of persons to answer the needs of the time. Few individuals can afford the cost and the time of such in-depth, careful preparation for ministry as can those of religious communities. Rather than a luxury, such training is urgent necessity for mission, for co-creating a new world.

Finally, vowed celibacy has important truth to offer about love, especially in our world today. What would happen if celibate persons learned to love intimately in ways not reduced to genital sexual expression? In other words, what would happen if a group of people really learned how to love each other in a world where the immediate expression of any kind of attraction or of affection is a genital sexual expression? What we would find, I suspect, is not a negation of love but rather a completion — one which brings others to life rather than using them, dominating them, intimidating them. Celibacy in community and in mission can lead to a discovery of the wonder of friendship — something our world knows only too little. Nonviolent, disarmed friendship is the key and the model for a peaceful world. The ultimate compliment that Jesus pays the persons who follow him is "I call you friends" (Jn 15:15). His command is to love one another (Jn 13:34). What would a celibate community mean to the world if its members unabashedly and unashamedly loved one another, sacrificed for one another, accepted one another in their weakness and in their vision?

Ultimately, celibacy must be profoundly connected and unified with the love of Jesus Christ — not a Jesus Christ who is a substitute for another husband, but Jesus Christ who is saviour, redeemer, bringer of the kingdom, and friend. Celibacy, I am convinced, means a personal, intimate knowledge of the person of Jesus Christ, for it is that knowledge which leads to life. In the stories of our beginnings as human beings, we see the understanding that God had created and, in that creation, was closely allied with humankind. Men and women could walk in the garden with their God. It is truly tragic that persons feel the need to hide from God, as did our ancestors.

The prophet Ezekiel talks about a God who walks along, and sees Israel lying in her own blood, picks her up and washes her off, makes her to grow and be beautiful (16:6-14). Jeremiah promises a new covenant that will be written on the heart, and everyone will know God (31:31-34). Hosea recalls for us a God who says: "How can I give you up, O Ephraim! How can I hand you over, O Israel! ... My heart recoils within me, my compassion grows warm and tender" (12:8). This is the omnipotent God to whom religious have vowed celibacy. The relationship between this God and the people has always been one that is marked by unswerving love, forgiveness, mercy.

The Incarnation tells us that the destiny of humankind is to be one with God in a way that is so profound and intimate that we have spent two thousand years just trying to figure out how to word it. The reason for these struggles is that it is beyond our wildest imaginations — what God has done with/for humankind. The Gospel of John tells us that eternal life is to know God and to know the one that God has sent (17:3). Knowledge for John is union; eternal life is fullness of life now. Ultimately, celibacy in community for mission must find its meaning in that union in order to receive there wholeness and life. Then vowed celibacy can say — in truth — that it is not the same as having a career, as being a single woman.

Is not *the* eschatological sign for our world a deep, personal knowledge of the divine? A knowledge that continuously deepens in terms of revelation of who God is. A revelation that comes to us in the very experiences and people of community and of mission. A knowledge which is integrated in prayer and which overflows in a life that is gladly given for others. A life that makes others come to their own life.

Obedience, Power and Authority

Within the context of individual perfection achieved primarily by means of removal from the world, obedience has primarily focused on denial of self and abnegation of one's own will in imitation of Jesus Christ who was obedient unto death (Phil 2:8). This form of obedience was expressed in absolute obedience to the religious superior, who was seen as Christ on earth. Superiors were above others and were to be treated as such. Most religious superiors never viewed themselves in such a way, it is undeniably true. However, the office of superior and the stringent requirements of a hierarchically structured understanding of one's vow of obedience required faithful acceptance of the requests, decisions, and sometimes orders of another "higher" person. The very title "superior" implies that others were "inferior."

A rigidly structured perception of obedience was not limited to religious congregations. Rather, religious received such a perception from the larger Church. They also returned this mentality to that Church. Obedience placed the burdens of decision-making upon a small group of individuals, while it left the way open for misunderstanding, misinterpretation and even misuse of roles and offices. Within such a context, dis-obedience was a very serious, a very wrong thing. For those who were called to obey —often without a "murmur" (as one Constitutions put it), questioning the accepted voices of authority was — and is — a difficult and somehow incorrect thing. This dynamic explains a great deal of the difficulty experienced by religious today.

Years of training, decades of faithful obedience have made it extremely painful to question points of view other than our own, particularly when these viewpoints are expressed by the persons to whom we have traditionally pledged our obedience. At the same time, our lived experience, our struggles to hear and speak the call of God's Spirit in these our times have led many to new viewpoints, to new ways of understanding. Yet, it is hard for the obedient, even though they are convinced of the value of their intentions, even to appear disobedient. How can those who sought abnegation of self for so long begin to assert themselves in ways that are creative, life-giving and holy?

Cultural Influences

The cultural influences upon our understanding of obedience do not provide much help in answering the foregoing question. Obedience is a dynamic reality, one which always involves a relationship between at least two persons. In contemporary culture, this dynamic is primarily one of manipulation. Obedience serves as a way to get persons or groups to do what someone else wants them to do. The dynamic expresses itself through the threat of punishment: "If you do not do this, severe consequences are in store for you." It finds expression in violence, several kinds of violence. There is the physical violence which fills our streets, our schools, our homes. There is also the violence of untruth. One withholds or distorts information which would enable others to make a free decision.

Getting others to do what we want them to do, whether it is good for them or not, obedience, as manipulation of others, finds its ultimate expression in war. The dynamic of force and of violence which all too often characterizes individual, group relationships now functions on the international, global scale. When a nation chooses a course other than what is deemed desirable by another nation, the tendency to resort to armed force is all too strong. "We will force you to do what we want or we will destroy you," is the threat which hovers in the air that all of us breathe each day. Obedience, which functions in superior-inferior relationships, usually fosters mistrust, rigidity, manipulation, and ultimately rebellion. At the heart of this understanding of obedience, lies a search for, and a protection of, power.

Sacred Scripture and Tradition

Obedience and power are inextricably linked. As one views the latter, so one expects the former to function. Scripture and tradition have much to say to us concerning both concepts and their interrelationship. One of the contemporary insights, which comes to us from the community of the faithful, is that of Mary Daniel Turner, S.N.D. de N.'s study of the meaning of power.[1] She defines power as energy, "energy as it comes to be by means of the dialectic between obedience and authority."[2] Authority, she says, is the capacity of a person to author a life's vision. Obedience is the commitment to fidelity to the vision. When one authors a meaningful vision for life, and when one remains faithful to that, energy is released. One becomes powerful. This is clearly a different understanding of power than the "fixed amount" clearly limited, a held-only-by-a-few version of power, which predominates in our world!

[1] Mary Daniel Turner, SNDdeN, "On Becoming Religious," *Starting Points: Six Essays Based on the Experience of U.S. Women Religious,* Lora Ann Quinonez, CDP, Ed. (Washington, D.C.: Leadership Conference of Women Religious, 1980), pp. 45-58.

[2] *Ibid.*, p. 49.

The dialectic between obedience and authority is profoundly related to the divine-human dialectic, according to Turner. It finds its source in creation itself. In creation, God empowers for life and offers humankind freedom from sin in the person of Jesus Christ. Our capacity to author, to co-create, begins in God's own creation. Such a capacity is shaped by contemplation. Contemplation is the ability to see in God's terms, to view the world and ourselves in the light of God's vision. Within this context, one is continually called to conversion. Such conversion leads us ever closer to communion — among ourselves and with the divine. Obedience,authority, power; creation, contemplation, conversion ... one is led to recall the ancient and wonderful image of the Trinity as continuous, life-giving dance.

As poverty cannot be confined to individual poverty, but rather involves corporate expression, so too obedience/power. What is corporate power and how is it related to obedience? Corporate power, according to Turner, is the commitment to the ongoing re-creation of a corporate vision to which the members of the group commit themselves. For most religious this has been expressed recently in the various processes involved in the wording of our Constitutions. Commitment to the on going re-creation of a corporate vision implies several things. First of all, it is necessary for each person to know her/himself intimately; and to know what our own personal visions are. Secondly, it is crucial that the members of the group are enabled to reverence the mystery that each person is. The corporate vision emerges from the revelation of the many individual visions. Reverence, then, is fundamental if the vision of another is to be truly seen. Thirdly, both the individual and the group must be willing to own what in both personal and corporate lives images God in the likeness of Jesus, or fails to image the divine. In other words, "What in my life, what in our life is true to the vision? What is not? What speaks to the world of the reign of God? What denies that reign?"

Obedience, within this context, is primarily understood as fidelity. To be obedient demands that one uses all of one's capacities, that one creates. Further, being obedient calls for contemplation and continual conversion. Being obedient together means calling forth each person's gifts, reverencing each one's mystery, acknowledging and transforming each one's blurred sight. Rather than force or violence, such obedience functions as prayer and as affirmation. Truly obedient people are not submisssive, they are powerful.

The scriptures, particularly as they speak to us of Jesus, have a great deal to tell us of power and authority and obedience. The gospels speak to us of Jesus' vision when they tell us that Jesus proclaimed the kingdom of God. Luke's gospel elaborates that vision in chapter 4, the scene of the inauguration of the ministry of the Messiah:

> The Spirit of the Lord is upon me and has anointed me to preach good news to the poor. The Spirit has sent me to proclaim release to the captives and recovering of sight to the blind, to set at liberty those who are oppressed, to proclaim the acceptable year of the Lord. (Lk 4:18-19)

After citing the wondrous promise of Isaiah, Jesus sat down (thus assuming the position of authority) and declared, "Today this scripture has been fulfilled in your hearing" (4:21). When he said this, Jesus claimed Isaiah's vision as his own and promised all who heard him that — in his person — the vision was to be realized. The entire ministry of Jesus, including his death and resurrection, witnesses to Jesus' fidelity to that vision. Further, the consistent compassion with which Jesus carried out his ministry give evidence of a contemplation which saw the world and its people as God saw them — in mercy and forgiveness. Thus Jesus cries out to the poor that they are blessed, to the hungry that they shall be fed, to the sinners that they are forgiven. His actions show the power which results from fidelity to vision.

Jesus came to do the will of God, to liberate and to give life, to bring people together in communion. The gospels tell us that his fidelity was the result of continuous, conscious choice. The temptation scene (Mt 4:1-11; Lk 4:1-13) makes that clear. Jesus was presented with certain ways of exercising power. He chose not to act in ways that were vainglorious or dominating, but rather to reveal the power of God's reign, the power of love. The passion predictions remind us that Jesus consciously *chose* to remain faithful to the vision, even when the consequences of his fidelity were so ominous. Further, he remained faithful to the vision even when that vision stood in apparent conflict with the exigencies of the Law. Thus, we find him accepting the presence of women in places where women were not "acceptable," eating with sinners, not insisting that his disciples fast while the "bridegroom" was with them. Jesus' ministry is power made visible, and it shows us what the true dialectic between authority and obedience looks like. Little wonder that we are told repeatedly that he taught with authority.

The authority with which Jesus taught had concrete ramifications in the lives of those who heard him. The power of Jesus led to conversion, to healing and to life. Jesus healed and he brought to life. Perhaps healing and bringing to life are the true criteria of gospel power! Jesus, further, freed others and enabled them to claim his vision as their ultimate priority, even when it was sometimes very difficult for them to do so within their own cultural context. At that time, women would not have appeared at the banquet table except to serve there. And, yet, over and over again we are told about women such as the Canaanite mother, women of poor reputation, a woman with an extremely expensive container of perfumed oil who defied criticism, disregarded the rules in order to get near to Jesus, to serve him, to anoint him, to obtain healing for those whom they loved. One becomes convinced that there must have been something so very appealing and inviting about the person of Jesus, that no one was afraid to approach him, to run the risks implied in drawing near to this powerful one.

This manifestation of power in approachability allowed others, not only to approach him but also to draw near to each other. Gospel authority inevitably leads to communion. When Jesus healed people, the result was not simply that one who could not previously walk was now able to leap with joy. Rather, the woman with a hemorrhage did not need to consider herself (or be considered) unclean anymore. The lepers no longer had to cower on the wrong side of the street. They could belong again to their community. The illnesses, which had kept them outside, which had ostracized them, were also healed. Jesus' healing always led to communion. His power, made manifest in his ministry, is the invasion of the reign of God into human history. It is a power which results from fidelity to the vision of that reign, which energizes in order to be, which leads to the communion which is the early Christian community.

The classic text to which we have referred for centuries, as we sought to understand obedience, is the beautiful Philippian hymn (Phil 2:5-11). That text urges the community to have among themselves the "mind" of Christ who humbled himself and became obedient "unto death, even death on a cross" (2:8). When the Philippians (and we) are urged to have the "mind" of Christ, perhaps they (and we) are exhorted to share in his vision and to cling in tenacious fidelity to that vision. The hymn reminds us that such fidelity will lead in the same way that it led the Christ, for the vision is no more popular, no less threatening in our time than it was in his.

The early Christian community consisted of the disciples who "caught" his vision and who continued his work. We are told in the New Testament that these power-less people were endowed with his own power. The community lived in communion — among themselves, and with Jesus in his Spirit. The Spirit of Jesus manifested itself and the continuation of Jesus' power among the people. The term *dunamis*, so frequently used in reference to the Spirit, implies energy, power, ... dynamite! The community, which lived in the Spirit and continued Jesus' ministry, were empowered to proclaim the Gospel. They shared the good news of God's reign. Such good news, we are told, is in itself a power for salvation (Rom 1:16). In the proclamation, the power of God is made manifest and, in turn, this power establishes the believers within that power.

The proclamation of the good news is a continuation of Jesus' vision; it is inviting all who hear to enter into the reign of God, to be energized and enabled by the spirit of Jesus. The power, set forth in proclamation, not only enables fidelity and courage; it also creates communion. Disciple-ship is marked not only by wondrous deeds and great good news, but also by the growth of community. Communion among believers is integral to the vision of God's reign. Within communion, the power of God is made manifest; hope and perseverance are created; unimaginable things happen. Ephesians says it well:

> For this reason I bow my knees before the Father, from whom every family in heaven and on earth is named, that according to the riches of God's glory, God may grant you to be strengthened with *power* through the Spirit in the inner person, and that Christ may dwell in your hearts through faith, that you, being rooted and grounded in love, may have the *power* to comprehend with all the saints what is the breadth and length and height and depth, and to know the love of Christ which surpasses knowledge, that you may be filled with all the fulness of God.
>
> Now to the one who by the *power* at work within us is able to do far more abundantly than all that we ask or think, to that one be glory in the church and in Christ Jesus to all generations, for ever and ever. Amen. (Eph 3:14-21)

The power spoken of in this text, is one which strengthens, which enables understanding, which is at work in us, is the power of which Turner speaks when she describes the dialectic between authoring a vision and remaining faithful to it in an ongoing relationship that is both personal and communal. Viewing obedience primarily in terms of unlimited, unrestricted power is certainly not the usual focus. Such focus, however, brings us closer to the gospel and maybe even closer to each other. Power, authority, and obedience, are deeply connected with each other, with God, with the action of God in our lives and in all of creation. In face of a culture which uses power to oppress or to bring death, the Christian understanding is one which brings to life, to enablement, to energizing.

Personal Experience

All of us have experienced power which can be oppressive, which is really violence. All of us long for the power which gives life, which unbinds and sets free. Within religious communities in the United States, expressions of the latter form of power have begun to emerge. One such expression is the participative structures within congregations. Such structures facilitate the sharing of all in the authoring of the common vision. They also enable all members to share in the understanding of the vision, to commit themselves to fidelity. Struggles to learn the art of communal discernment, working toward consensus among ourselves, these are conscious (and sometimes difficult) efforts to word a vision together. One of the realities which has become more and more clear to us is the asceticism of communal discernment. It is very difficult for peoples trained in the search for THE truth, to leave their own conviction that they know THE truth, and to join with others in prayer and hope in order to allow God's truth to emerge in our midst. Corporate obedience such as this requires patience, trust and constant attentiveness to the surprise that is the power of God's spirit.

Corporate obedience always reaches out beyond the confines of the particular group, and shows itself in the way that a group seeks to relate with others. Thus, those who seek participation and collaboration among themselves, also seek these same ideals among the peoples with whom they live and serve. Relationships are marked by mutuality and reverence, rather than competition or domination. They are also characterized by common searching for the vision, common fidelity to God's reign.

Much of our experience is expressed in symbolic action. It has become most common for us to gather together in circles (although we may sometimes feel that we go around in circles!). We take our places at round tables; we join hands in a circle when we pray or celebrate. This fact is not without meaning for the circle implies collaboration, room for expansion, ability to see each other, mobility to dance in celebration. One does not climb the ladder of success or move to the front of the line; rather, one joins with others, and therein finds cause for celebration.

A contemporary expression of an ancient tradition speaks, perhaps, most eloquently of the obedient life in our times. Several years ago, I had the happy opportunity to be in Barcelona, Spain on a Sunday morning. My companion and I had heard of the beauty of the Catalan folk dances which were performed each Sunday in Barcelona. We were told that these dances — which were at that time against the law — were held each Sunday afternoon in the plaza in front of the Cathedral. We made plans to visit another sight in the morning, and to go to the Cathedral in the afternoon.

The porter at our hotel (who had seen us through many a communications problem) informed us that we should go to the Cathedral in the morning. We explained that we would go in the afternoon. "You will go in the morning," he said. And so, obediently, we went in the morning. When we arrived at the Cathedral, we found ourselves among hundreds of Catalan people who had come to dance unannounced, illegal dances.

The instruments were very old; the dancers were of all ages. The dance itself was a circle dance. There were "circles" of two and circles of fifty. One circle consisted of a very young man and a very old, old gentleman. Another was comprised of grandparents teaching toddlers the dance and, in the dance, their heritage. But it is in the steps of the dance that one sees a vision of power and obedience and authority.

When the dance begins, a circle is formed; the dancers join hands, arms at their sides. As the dance progresses, there are moments when the joined hands are lowered, and others when they are raised high in the air. If someone wishes to join the dance, she must wait until the hands are lowered and then, bending low, must pass under the hands into the center of the circle. Once there, persons must leave something of themselves on the ground. We watched mothers set their babies there, young women their coats or purses. Men put their briefcases or wallets. Couples left the baby's stroller. All of these were meant to symbolize the giving of oneself to the group. When this has been done, the arms of the circle are raised in celebration and the person takes his/her place in the dance.

People faithful to a vision, true to their heritage are not afraid to join hands, to bow, to leave their possessions in the midst of the circle that is community. They are energetic people who dance together — even when it is illegal — and remember the vision. Perhaps a vowed life of obedience is most truly a life, which dances in celebration of God's vision, which does so in community and in trust. . . a dance which delights the dancers and gives new visions to all who are graced to see and perhaps join in.

The Vowed Life as Prophetic Ministry

Each of the vows has great significance; each has a long and varied history within the church. It must be remembered, however, that religious do not live the vows separately, but rather together in a vowed life. We must continually ask what the vowed life means, how it is an expression of the gospel, how it, in itself, is ministry in our world. There are multiple ways to do this and many images which can serve as context in which to elucidate the meaning and values of religious life. In his recent work, *Prophetic Imagination*,[1] I believe Walter Brueggemann suggests a context: that of prophetic ministry. I would like to summarize briefly how Brueggemann views such ministry and then relate that to what has been said concerning the vows.

Brueggemann states that the task of prophetic ministry is "to nurture, nourish, and evoke a consciousness and a perception alternative to the consciousness and perception of the dominant culture around us."(p. 13) The way prophetic ministry accomplishes its task is two-fold: it makes public the death and dying in the dominant culture; it energizes for a new vision of the alternative culture. Brueggemann traces the history of such ministry from Moses to Jesus. Moses' actions were responsible for the dismantling of the oppres-

---

[1] Walter Brueggemann, *The Prophetic Imagination*, Philadelphia: Fortress Press, 1978.

sive regime of the Pharaoh and the freeing of the people. His ministry really began in the groans and laments of the people, which he made public and, thus, "real." Moses also evoked the vision of an alternative when he voiced hymns of praise to the God who saved. The Mosaic tradition affirms three things which are basic to the prophetic , alternative community: "The alternative life is lived in this very particular historical and historicizing community. This community criticizes and energizes by its special memories that embrace discontinuity and genuine breaks from imperial reality. This community, gathered around the memories, knows it is defined by and is at the disposal of a God who as yet is unco-opted and uncontained by the empire." (p. 27) Thus, the alternative community lives in the midst of its world as both critic and energizer. Its point of reference, its identity is determined by the God who is free and who calls to freedom.

The monarchical period gave rise to stress on stifling criticism and denying energy for the sake of establishing stability. The aim was to create a sense that everything would continue forever as it was then. The prophet Jeremiah spoke in response to this mentality. He is what Brueggemann calls a prophet of radical criticism against the royal consciousness. Jeremiah's is a ministry of grief. He conjures up a funeral; he brings the grief of a dying Israel to public expression — in his words and his actions. Jeremiah, in his lament, brought to light that which the dominant culture sought to deny: its own death. He reminds us that life will not continue forever as those in power would like it to do.

Second Isaiah represents the other side of prophetic ministry for Brueggemann. To a people convinced that everything was over forever, this prophet speaks images of enthronement, new creation, new futures. In so doing, second Isaiah penetrates the despair of the people and energizes them to amazement.

In Jesus' ministry both aspects of prophetic ministry come to fulfilment. He laments the dying within the culture, the burdens laid upon people, the laws which place restrictions upon the healing power of God. The dismantling of the oppressive regime, foreshadowed in Moses, is fully wrought in Jesus' crucifixion. In his death, the oppression and violence which killed Jesus were themselves defeated by resurrection. Jesus amazed and energized those who heard him for he evoked visions of a different future. In his future, the poor know theirs is the kingdom, sinners are forgiven, the hungry fed, the lame walk, widows regain their sons. In the resurrection Jesus embodies the new future given by God. His story tells us that, in our own stories, violence and oppression will not endure forever; life and hope are never ended forever — even in the face of death.

To view the vowed life within this context is to suggest possibilities which are indeed amazing. How can this life exercise the ministry of grief and that of energizing to amazement? A few suggestions:

The vow of poverty is a critique of all in our culture that declares poverty and the poor to be immoral, less than fully human. The choice of this vow, as we have described it, can be a very healthy criticism of the American myth that one must climb the ladder and reach the top. It is a question to the sense of helpessness and worthlessness that permeates much of our society. Very few ever reach the tops of ladders; those below all too frequently stand in silent misery and feel themselves to be failures. What if those who choose poverty took the misery into themselves, and gave it expression in the public forum? At the same time, living the vow can energize to amazement by sharing, by hearing, by valuing the devalued in our world. When we own our human poverty, its ambiguity, its potential for redemption, we provide an alternative consciousness to our world. Poverty, chosen for the kingdom, energizes and amazes when it is enfleshed as good news to the poor, as revelation of God's reign in our midst.

Obedience, correctly understood in terms of the dialectic between authoring a vision and fidelity to that vision, decries the death of our time, when it denies the power struggles that are in every aspect of life. Such obedience grieves publicly over abused power, which leads to oppression and war. If we truly lived obedience, would we not lament violence, the abuse of persons, the immediate resort to force and intimidation in all arenas, even those of our own congregations and the institutional church? Clearly such obedience energizes to amazement, for it calls forth that power which is energy. It enables people to author their visions, to rejoice in the new future promised in those visions. Can obedience energize to amazement by reminding the world of the power that is Jesus Crucified, a power which leads to community, and which brings people together — not apart? Any groups which bring people to their own power, which struggle to collaborate and learn together rather than to win, are certainly amazing!

Vowed celibacy laments the dying in our culture. It grieves over the use of people; it makes public the terrible loneliness and void which are present in twentieth century civilization. It denounces the degradation of human sexuality, and especially the degradation of women that is so deeply entrenched in all of us. It makes public the tragedy of peoples scurrying every-which-way, looking for something — anything — to muffle their needs for love, for intimacy. Celibacy truly energizes when it gives sustained witness to love that is *for* people, rather than false love which uses people and is ultimately *against* them. The community which celebrates its poverty and rejoices in its vision, which affirms women as whole persons, which strives for communion not only with its own members but with its brothers and sisters everywhere is a wondrous, miraculous alternative. Can religious energize in a single-hearted, large-hearted love, which brings the kingdom to life and brings lives into the kingdom?

Life lived this way is prophetic ministry, and prophetic ministry is a way of life. It permeates all that we do, and it does so with both pain and joy. To allow our commitment to take us into the very heart of the world is to open ourselves to all that is dying, to all that kills. It is, in a very real sense, to dive into an overwhelming sea of anguish. It is not enough to attack that anguish or the causes of it in our world. The prophetic minister is called to *share* the suffering and to let her/his cry rise from the depths of the people's lament. The prophetic minister is called to dive into the sea of anguish and *not to drown*, but rather to find in its very depths the gift and the promise of new life. Doxology must accompany lamentation. The future, which God wills, becomes visible in the song of the prophetic ministers. The wonderful alternatives are played out in their lives. How many people in the nuclear age really, confidently believe in the future? Belief in a wonderful future is the very cornerstone of prophetic ministry *and* of vowed commitment.

All Christians are called to prophetic ministry, each according to her/his own gifts. The gift of vowed religious is to live such ministry by means of a vowed life in community, so that the specific contributions such a life can make are given freely to our sisters and brothers and all, together, are led to the unveiling of the kingdom of God among us.

I began this essay with a word about the importance of language, and the different functions which language can perform. I stated that it is my belief that the language which most expresses our times is "parable-language." Parables speak of a time when old worlds are disrupted and new, unexpected ones come to be — ones of blessing and of life, of song and of surprise. I would end what is only a beginning reflection with another parable.

"He told them another parable. The kingdom of heaven is like leaven which a woman took and hid in three measures of flour, till it was all leavened" (Mt 13:33).

This parable, like all parables, is marvelously illogical. In the first place, Jesus tells us that in the kingdom of heaven it's like what a *woman* does. Secondly, it's like a woman who takes some leaven to make some bread; but, we must remember that leaven was not such a good thing to those who heard the parable. The disciples are warned to beware of the leaven of the Pharisees and Sadducees (Mt 16:6 and //). Paul, referring to the Judaic commands concerning unleavened bread, urges the Corinthians to celebrate the festival "with the unleavened bread of sincerity and truth" (1

Cor 5:8). The kingdom of heaven is like a person who takes something not normally viewed as good, and puts it into the bread. Thirdly, the amount of bread this woman made would equal approximately 300 loaves today. No woman would bake 300 loaves of bread in her kitchen . . . unless her kitchen happened to be a commercial bakery! The parable tells us that the way it works when God reigns, is like the wrong person using the wrong thing and ending up with a banquet.

Today religious are in parable time. There is much that seems negative, much that has disappeared, much that has suddenly appeared. Parable time is time of surprise. Perhaps all that seems so painful, so illogical, might just surprise us. Perhaps we shall discover that, unknowingly, we've prepared a feast and the bounty of the feast just might feed the world.

Authority in the Church:
Biblical Foundations
Anthony   Kosnik

Authority is a difficult concept to define, especially so, when one attempts to unravel from biblical sources its basic meaning and draw out some implications for the exercise of church authority. One of the reasons is that there are many and important variations in meaning. What is noticeable from the very outset, is that the New Testament writers avoid or only very rarely use words which signify authority in terms of "power" in the classical Greek or secular sense, that is, in the sense of: to govern, to rule, to command, to order. The word, "hierarchy," which we almost automatically connect with authority, is not found in the New Testament. "*Arche*," a word that symbolizes ruling power-authority in the sense of domination and control —occurs ten times, but it is never applied to authority in the church. "*Taxis*" is another word that has similar connotations and also appears ten times, but is never applied to the kind of authority that Christ was sharing with his apostles. The word that is most frequently used in those passages that are translated as authority in the New Testament, is the Greek word "*exousia*" which appears some ninety-five times and is often connected with situations where it is indicated that

Christ teaches with authority, with *"exousia."* He has been commissioned, has been sent; he has power from the Father. This same word is used where the Scriptures speak of Christ's authority; that he has power to forgive sins; that he is called Lord of the Sabbath; that he has the power to work miracles or to cast out demons. Most significantly, it is used to describe Christ's teaching and preaching — so different from that of the rabbis. Christ is called the Teacher, because he teaches not as the rabbis of his time did, but as one who preaches with authority. It is the same word that is used when the Bible speaks of the conflict that Christ encountered when he went about doing his work — often times in violation of the law of his day — the Sabbath, the purification laws, or even when working his miracles. His enemies begin to question him: "By whose authority are you doing these things?" (Mt. 21:24). Christ never answered that question directly. He threw the question back at his attackers by asking them: "By whose authority did John the Baptist do his preaching?" (Mt. 21:25) — a question that his enemies would not answer because they knew that they would entrap themselves.

The New Testament, read carefully, indicates that the Christians of that era knew only one authority, one head of the church and that was Jesus Christ. He appointed no successor with that fullness and absoluteness of authority that was his. As McKenzie writes: "Christ never left the church — not even today."[1] And so the center of gravity around which the Scriptures revolve is not really the question of authority but the enduring life of Christ among his people — that mission which he shared with his apostles and commissioned them to carry out: to preach the Good News, to share the Kingdom, to go and teach all nations, and baptize them in the name of the Father, and of the Son, and of the Holy Spirit. In commissioning his apostles to do that, Christ did give some very clear observations about how he expected them to behave. He gave them what we would call

[1]McKenzie, John L. *Authority in the Church.* 1966. p. 21.

:re is one image or one word that best sum-
.st had to say on the subject it would be the
:." It is a word that is frequently translated
ꞇ its more common and existential meaning
in those times, and certainly in terms of Christ's intention,
ought more properly be translated "slave." The only passage
in the New Testament where Jesus summarized his whole
ministry in one sentence is found at the end of the dispute
concerning the rank and place and glory which the disciples
will have. You can recall the scene: the loving concern of the
mother of the sons of Zebedee about the welfare of her sons,
bold enough to approach Christ and ask a special place for
them in the kingdom. Christ answers that he cannot assure
them that place. He assures them only that they will have to
bear the chalice of suffering. The attempt, however, resulted
in a dispute among the apostles. The Gospel says: "The
other ten on hearing this became indignant with the two
brothers." Jesus then called them together. "You know how
those who exercise authority among the Gentiles lord it over
them. Their great ones make their importance felt. It cannot
be like that with you. Anyone among you who aspires to
greatness must serve the needs of all. Such is the case with
the Son of Man, who has come not to be served by others
but to serve. To give his own life as a ransom for many"
(Mk. 10:41 ff).

It is true that the word "diakonos" did have many meanings even in New Testament times. It could be translated
with the meaning of "service" in the modern sense, but then
much of the force of the original meaning would be watered
down and lost — at least the meaning that Christ intended
to give it. From this text and from the other instances where
Christ uses the word in sharing with his apostles it would
seem better translated as "slave" or "lackey." We see Christ
at the Last Supper dramatically trying to communicate this
sense. How deeply he felt about the manner in which this
authority was to be exercised is cited in the Gospel of John.
It tells us that Jesus, fully aware that he had come from God
and was going to God, rose from the meal and took off his

cloak. He picked up the towel and tied it around himself and then he poured water into a basin and began to wash his disciples' feet, and dry them with the towel he had around him. "Do you understand what I just did for you? You address me as teacher and lord, and fittingly enough, for that is what I am. But I washed your feet, I who am teacher and lord. And if I, who am teacher and lord, wash your feet, then you must wash each other's feet. What I just did was give you an example. As I have done, so you must do. I solemnly assure you, no slave is greater than his master, no messenger out-ranks the one who sent him. Once you know all these things, blessed will you be if you put them into practice" (John 13:13 ff). Here is the key that provides the solution to the authority question — if only all of us in the Church could put it into practice!

On still another occasion, we find Jesus telling his disciples that if they wish to get into the Kingdom of Heaven, they must become as little children. The greatest among them must become like a small child. These expressions of slave and child are more than conventional exhortations to some mundane kind of humility. Children and slaves in ancient times were not bearers of authority. Under most of the prevailing laws, they weren't even persons. And so very, very effectively and pointedly, Christ's answer to the question: "Who is the greatest among you? Who is in authority? Who has power?" is NO ONE! No one! The secular models of authority find no place in the New Testament!

From the opening temptation in the desert to the closing scene in Gethsemane, Christ rejected the kind of authority that speaks of power, domination, force and oppression. He rejects outright Satan's offer of power over the masses that would greatly simplify his task of reconciling humankind. He rebukes Peter's attempt to use force to protect him indicating that he could command legions of angels if he so wished. The authority with which Christ speaks and to which he calls his disciples has nothing to do with the secular, political, worldly notion of authority.

There is yet another image that is used in Scripture to describe the kind of authority that Christ wants for his church. It is the notion of "shepherd" that appears in the gospel of John — chapter 10 — the description of the Good Shepherd. "I am the good shepherd who lays down his life for his sheep. No one takes it from me. I lay it down freely. I have power to lay it down and take it up again. This command I have received from my Father." This is one of the very few places where John uses the word "authority" in his gospel. He uses that word to account for the fact that Jesus acknowledges that he received from the Father the authority to yield his own life, by his own free decision, and not by exterior coercion or violence. It is true that even in the New Testament, the symbol "shepherd" could be understood royally and politically. There are instances in the secular literature where kings would regard themselves as shepherds. The interesting difference is the way that it is used in the gospel of John. This shepherd is one who knows his sheep and is ready to lay down his life for those sheep. It is this sense of complete and total giving of self in genuine service and total commitment to the building, caring and nourishing of the community that Christ has in mind when he speaks of authority. This focus and emphasis which Christ gives to authority is quite different from the political and secular understanding of the word.

But did the early church understand and exercise authority in this sense? One of the key questions that we need to ask is: Did Christ really establish a hierarchically ordered church? Is that the kind of power, the kind of authority, that he wished his disciples to establish and to operate under. Historical evidence indicates quite convincingly that hierarchical ordering of the church, as we know it today, from the papacy to the bishops to the priests to the deacons, really did not come into the church before the second century. If Christ intended and ordered that kind of church, evidently the apostles did not hear very well and did not respond. A closer examination of scripture indicates that if we make that kind of division between the rulers and the ruled,

between shepherds who govern and sheep who follow, we
are misunderstanding the kind of authority and power that
Christ did commit to his followers.

The missionary discourse, recorded in all three synoptic
Gospels and intended not just for leaders but for all who
were to become his disciples deserves some reflection. In all
three accounts, the power of going forth to teach, the power
of proclaiming the Good News that the Kingdom is here, the
advice on how they are to conduct themselves, the stern
prohibition against gathering material resources for themselves, and the entrusting of unbelievers to the judgment of
God are common elements. Matthew reports "And he
summoned his *twelve* disciples. . . " (Mt. 9:1, 2). In Luke it
says: "the Lord appointed *seventy-two* and sent them in
pairs before him to every town and place he intended to
visit" (Luke 10:1). If some in the early church attempted to
restrict this mission to the twelve or to the apostles, Luke
found it necessary to correct and rectify this misconception.
In his recounting of that mission statement it is recognized
that the mission was given to all of Christ's followers and
not just to those we call the twelve.

An even more convincing passage is the text in Matthew
that speaks of the promise to Peter: "Thou art Peter and
upon this rock I will build my church and the gates of hell
shall not prevail against it. I will entrust to you the keys to
the Kingdom of Heaven so that whatever you declare bound
on earth shall be bound in Heaven; and whatever you
declare loosed on earth, shall be loosed in Heaven" (Mt.
16:18-20). This text is one that has often been used as the
basis for papal and church authority, and for the kind of
organizational hierarchy that we experience in the church.
As one scripture commentator remarks: "One has to marvel
at the reasoning by which a rock and the keys become
full-fledged juridical power defined in purely political
terms."[2] If we look at that text in all three synoptics we find

2McKenzie, op. cit. p. 41

that all three report Peter's profession of faith — his recognition that Christ is the Messiah, the Son of God! Through the revelation of the Father, Peter has an insight into the Messiahship of Jesus, and that insight he expresses in his act of faith. What is interesting is that neither Mark nor Luke follow that act of profession with the power of the keys. Much of early biblical commentary, even up to St. Thomas in the Middle Ages, did not understand this particular text as an authorization by Christ to establish the power of jurisdiction in a political sense. The whole thrust of the text is that it is the kind of faith that Peter has professed, that Christ wishes to make the basis and foundation of his church. It is that kind of faith on which the church can rest securely. The rock, in other words, upon which the church rests, is not a person but it is the kind of faith that Peter gives example to — not understood personally, but as embodying the kind of faith upon which the church must depend for the fulfillment of the mission.

The metaphor of the keys is perhaps the clearest symbol of authority that we find in the scriptures. Secular texts confirm the interpretation that the metaphor of the keys is meant to symbolize the communication of authority. Keys make one master of the house. Jesus could not have said more clearly that Peter becomes the master of the palace of the church in this symbol of handing over of the keys. But if the term is analyzed further, it means that Peter had the management of the domestic affairs of the church. And here we run the danger of pressing this metaphor too far because the kind of authority that Christ communicated to his followers and to Peter must always be understoood in terms of the church's mission of proclaiming and baptizing. To specify beyond this is to do something which the gospel text itself does not do, and, which we will see, the New Testament experience does not do. What this means is that the jurisdictional management of the church in the political sense is something that Christ has almost nothing to say about and leaves open to development.

Even the commission given to Peter and John after the

resurrection is one that is based on Peter's love for Jesus. Peter is asked to prove his love by carrying out the mission and by feeding the flock. If his love for Jesus is genuine, he will direct it in service to those who have been entrusted to his care as shepherd. In the image of "shepherd" we have a term indicating authority but an authority that is far removed from ideas of domination and control. It is an authority of love, of service, of nourishment, and of direction in faith from those whose first care is the flock for which Jesus died, and for whom the shepherd must be ready to die. This is the way the early church understood Christian leadership. The dominant ideas are leadership in faith and love with no particular details of governance even hinted at.

How did the New Testament Church implement this idea of authority and service to God's people? It might be well to begin with the person of Peter. There can be no question that Peter held a special place of leadership in the apostolic church. It is obvious from many texts in scripture that he is the spokesman for the group at its own meetings especially in Acts 1-11 where the early development of the church is recorded. It is Peter who takes the lead in the proclamation of the Gospel. It is he who appears before the Jewish council to defend their right to preach. It is he who in their gathering initiates the election of Matthias, and it is he who begins the mission to the Gentiles. It is interesting that Peter's preeminence and prominence in these first twelve chapters is as noticeable as is his absence afterwards.

Can we say then with any certainty that Peter was recognized as having universal and immediate jurisdiction over the whole church? At the First Jerusalem Council (Acts 15) Peter is only one of the speakers in favor of the decision that was finally adopted by the group. Paul, in his letter to the Galatians, certainly recognized Peter as one of the pillars of the Jerusalem Church; but there is no hard evidence that Peter was actually either Bishop of Jerusalem or Bishop of Rome. In an interesting ecumenical study directed by Raymond Brown, some of the best contemporary Catholic and Protestant scripture scholars reached the conclusion that there is no clear and specific evidence in scripture for the Petrine office as we have come to know and understand it. This office is a later development and it is unfair to read into the text of scripture the kind of understanding of that office that evolved only in time.

Paul certainly does not regard himself as head of the church, but he does create a problem because he recognizes no one else as head. He is very careful to remain on good terms with the Jerusalem church. He wishes to leave no doubt that his gospel is identical with the gospel which is preached everywhere. But he recognizes no special obedience to central headquarters. He speaks on his own and he affirms that! Once he received his commission from the church of Antioch, he acts independently not even professing submission to the church of Antioch from which he came. His claim was that he was as much an apostle as anyone else.

It is obvious that Peter's leadership in the early church was anything but absolute. In Acts 1-12 where Peter's leadership is best seen and most explicitly articulated, Peter in no case acts on his own authority without consultation, without deliberation, without the consensus of the others. In the election of Matthias, although he initiates it, it is clear that the decision to elect a replacement for Judas by lot was the decision of the entire group.

In the instance where the Greeks complained about the fact that their widows were being neglected, the scriptures tell us "the twelve" assembled the community of disciples and said: "Look around among your own members for seven men acknowledged to be deeply spiritual and prudent and we shall appoint them to this task." The scriptures tell us the proposal was unanimously accepted by the community. This is hardly a heavy handed imposition by one person in the church. It was a communal decision with real authority delegated to the local level. It is a beautiful illustration of one of the fundamental principles of church governance called subsidiarity.

In another instance in the conversion of Samaria, the

scripture tells us: "When the apostles heard in Jerusalem that Samaria had accepted the Word of God, they sent Peter and John to them"(Acts 8:14). Can you imagine the College of Bishops sending John Paul II? It doesn't quite work that way today. Still another example — the baptism of Cornelius! Acts 11 informs us that the circumcised believers who accompanied Peter were surprised that the gifts of the Holy Spirit should have been poured out on the Gentiles. They could be heard speaking in tongues and glorifying God. And Peter, at that point, put the question: "What can stop these people who have received the Holy Spirit, even as we have, from being baptized by water?" Only after raising the question — and implicitly gaining consensus — does Peter proceed. Imagine yourself in that same scene. Evidently some of the circumcised had accompanied Peter, and in the house of Cornelius they observed Gentiles speaking in tongues and showing signs of having received the Spirit. The traditional Jews were finding it very hard, as we often did before Vatican II, to believe that the Spirit could operate any place but within the church. Their first reaction was one of opposition. Before Peter would move, he put the question to them: "What objections can we have if the Holy Spirit is operating"(Acts 10:47). Only then, do the scriptures tell us that he then gave orders that they be baptized in the name of Jesus Christ. And that wasn't the end of the controversy. When Peter returned to Jerusalem, some of the circumcised took issue with him: "You went to the house of the uncircumcised and ate with them. And then Peter explained the whole affair step-by-step from the beginning" (Acts 11). Peter was called to justify, to explain. He was called to accountability. He had to appear before the group and explain step-by-step the whole affair.

And when there was a famine occurring in some of the churches "the *disciples* determined to set something aside according to their means and to send it to the relief of the brothers who lived in Judea"(Acts 11:29). Even so minor a matter as taking up a collection was not a matter of direct order from on high but a matter of consensus decision among those early leaders of the church.

Finally, the account in Acts of the missioning of Barnabas and Paul, gives still another example of how authority was shared in the early church. "There were in the church at Antioch certain prophets and teachers: Barnabas, Simeon, Lucius of Cyrene, Manaen, and Saul. On one occasion when they were engaged in the Liturgy of the Word and were fasting, the Holy Spirit spoke to them: Set apart Barnabas and Saul for me to do the work for which I have called them. And then after they had fasted and prayed, they imposed hands on them and sent them off" (Acts 13).

The type of leadership expressed in the early church is best designated by a term which has become common in post-Vatican II terminology. It is known as "collegiality." It is authority exercised by the whole, the community working together — not just the Apostles — not just the disciples — but especially, this last text has indicated, all of those who are active in the mission of the church — prophets, teachers, wonder-workers, evangelists, presbyters and others. This is a clear indication that it was recognized in the early church that the Spirit, in fact, is given to the whole church and not exclusively to the leaders. The whole church has the commission, the responsibility, to proclaim the Good News. The Spirit gives to the church a great diversity of gifts and charisms and all must be brought together to work for the good of the whole. The power which Christian authority has is grounded in the Holy Spirit and that Holy Spirit is open to all. What conclusions can we draw from this New Testament evidence about ecclesial authority in the early New Testament church? As we have seen, authority in the church as it is described by Christ and exercised by the apostles is never understood as just another form of standard social or political authority. That notion is repeatedly rejected as unacceptable and unserviceable. The careful choice of the word "diakonos" in references to authority clearly indicates that the underlying characteristic of authority in the church is service.

Secondly, the authority, that the church has and experiences, must always be seen and understood in relation to its source — Jesus Christ! The Father has given Him all authority and after the Resurrection, Christ sent the Holy Spirit among his people with the promise that the Spirit would be there always. Hans Küng has an interesting commentary on what happens when we forget that Christ is head and assume his authority for our own. He writes: "The New Testament message gives no basis at all for the idea about the development of the church which plays down or even domesticates the idea of the reign of Christ. It is extremely misleading to speak of the church as the continuing life of Christ or as a permanent incarnation of Christ. For in such views the church is identified with Christ so that Christ as its Lord and Head takes second place to his church — the church which pretends to be the Christ of the present in constantly new incarnation." We will see in one of the later periods of the church that the notion of the papacy as the Vicar of Christ is so exalted that the theologians of that age begin to speak of a real presence of Christ under pontifical species! That's carrying the image a bit far!

In this distorted view Christ is seen as a constantly new incarnation. Christ has abdicated in favor of a church which has taken his place and become his autonomous representative in everything. And so the church has gone a long way toward making Christ superfluous. It does not deny Christ but on the contrary, affirms him by identifying itself with him. People have only to keep with the church and, thereby, will keep to Christ himself. How often have we seen that happen?

As a newly ordained young priest, I was absolutely convinced that, in a great many areas, by being faithful to the official church teaching I was doing nothing more than being faithful to Christ. On issues like divorce and remarriage, contraception, sterilization, sexuality, ecumenism and many others, I was doing nothing more than carrying out what Christ had clearly preached and what the church had faithfully practiced through an unbroken tradition of twenty centuries. I have to confess that my excessive fidelity to the teaching, to the rule, and to the order of the church did a great deal of harm. Though it was not my intention to do so, my zealousness had serious negative effects on the people I dealt with in the confessional, in counselling sessions, and in a great number of other situations. Thank God that many have come to realize that the church in its official teaching and governance is not always mirroring the presence of Christ. When one identifies Christ with the church, then a knowing church has replaced a believing church. A professing church has replaced a needing church. And total authority has replaced obedience. The church has become its own mistress, and it no longer needs a master. And the continuing Christ is responsible only to itself. Human commandments are turned into divine commandments. And such a church is a caricature of itself. Is there such a church? It would be hard to deny that such a church always exists at least as a temptation — a powerful temptation. The temptation to become an autonomous and an autocratic church which puts itself in the place of Christ. Historically we've learned that every time we've done that, we have known shipwreck. And the mission for which we have been called has not been furthered, realized or accomplished. And so, the point that the New Testament knew so clearly — that Christ was the source of authority against which all must be judged — is a crucial one for our understanding of authority in the early church.

A third point is that this authority which is rooted in Christ is always to be understood, interpreted, applied and exercised in relationship to the mission that Christ entrusted to his disciples. And that mission that we know from both Matthew and John and the other evangelists was the mission of baptizing and proclaiming the Good News to the ends of the earth. To read more into that mission in terms of governance is to read more into it than the New Testament evidence provides.

A fourth point, the exercise of authority in the church

ought to be an exercise in collegiality. It is not autocratic or autonomous or exercised out of touch with all who have been called the followers of Christ. It must be a collegial, communal and consensual exercise of leadership.

And fifthly, it is a servant authority. It consists of a spending of oneself to build the unity of God's people. The great variety of gifts given by the Spirit is intended and meant to be brought together to build the community of God's people, so that there will be one flock and one shepherd. And the role of shepherd is to be understood as a role of service and of sacrifice — even to the point of laying down one's life for the sheep.

Finally, there are precious few rules and directives in the New Testament regarding administrative authority! No one denies that that kind of authority is important and necessary for the effective carrying out of the mission. But it is clear from the New Testament that Christ did not touch the issue. It is one that he kept pretty much open to development and growth in response to the great variety of circumstances and needs that his apostles and disciples would encounter as they attempt to carry out the mission. Even in the New Testament churches themselves, we see a great variety of forms being developed in the Jerusalem and Pauline churches. Nor is this development closed with the apostolic age. It will continue to be changed and modified according to different circumstances and times and needs. Both the New Testament evidence and the continuing history of the church indicate that the form of administrative authority is open to continuous growth, development and change. It has always been changing — and more than ever it needs to be changed today. The fact that Christ left that open to change, and the fact that history has indicated constant change, is both basis and reason for hope that we can change the present form of exercising the political and administrative authority in the church to reflect more closely the way Christ and the early church exercised authority as a loving service — collegially exercised — to build up God's people — the church.

History and Development of Church Authority

We closed our last reflections on authority in the New Testament church by saying that the characteristics of this authority as it was exercised were: Christic, collegial, exercised on the local level, respecting the principle of subsidiarity, and directed to carrying out the mission, that is the upbuilding of the community that Christ called together.

We want now to look at what happened with that authority in the developing history of the church. We will move rather quickly through the early periods of church history until we come to our own modern day where I want to focus on authority, especially as reflected in the official documents of the church's magisterium. In the last twenty years we have been through some very important changes in the official church's self-understanding of that authority, as well as the manner of its exercise.

The first, second and third centuries were the time of persecutions in the church — the Age of Martyrs. In the writings of that early church, Yves Congar notes that the notion of authority that prevailed centered around three values: 1) the need for authority, 2) its collegial exercise and 3) its spiritual or charismatic quality.[1]

---

[1]Congar, Yves. "The Historical Development of Authority in the church" in *Problems of Authority* edited by John Todd. Helicon Press, 1962, pp. 119 ff.

There was in this period a very strong insistence on authority. By the start of the second century, we begin to find bishops overseeing the local churches. The jurisdictional authority that is required for a growing and developing community is being set in place. The bishops, as the leaders, speak very strongly about authority. Ignatius, for instance, writes: "Cling to your bishops, to the presbyterium, and to the deacons." These were the centers of unity of the early church. Their task was to keep the community together — a community that was constantly threatened under trial and often dispersed. Ignatius, the Martyr, sees the importance of having a rallying central point for the community that is the church. The great Bishop Cyprian provides what is probably the most frequently quoted expression from that era of the church when he says: "Where the bishop is, there is the church." The bishop is in the church, and the church is in the bishop.

Although the emphasis on authority is very strong and very clear, it is always in the context of an emphasis on the church, understood as the community of God's people — not in terms of hierarchy over the sheep but rather as one with and part of the community.

Cyprian, for instance, the same bishop who says: "The bishop is the church and the church is the bishop" writes: "I have made it a rule ever since my episcopate to make no decision merely on the strength of my own personal opinion without consulting you, the priests and deacons, and without the approbation of the people."[2] The collegiality that we saw in the early church, exercised by Peter and the apostles, continued to be a very strong characteristic of church authority even in the Age of Martyrs. The laity took part in the election of their bishops and chose their own ministers very much as in the New Testament, with the selection of deacons... "Seek among yourselves for people who are prudent and spiritual" (Acts 6:3). They supplied information for the councils. They shared in the establishment of

[2] Cyprian. Epist. 14:4

religious customs and church regulations which would order their lives. They had, in a word, a strong say in matters dealing with the administration of church affairs.

The third characteristic of the exercise of authority in that age was that it was marked by a strong spiritual or charismatic dimension. In other words, the emphasis was not heavily jurisdictional or legalistic. The bishops were chosen because they were the ones who exhibited outstanding charismatic gifts in that early community. They were chosen by the people because they were natural leaders. They were the ones who had the qualifications of spirituality and prudence that were most needed for keeping that early community centered and together. It is interesting to recall one of the practices of that early church which illustrates how this authority was marked by spirituality or charisma. When people, who were marked for martyrdom, survived their ordeal without denying their faith, they were recognized in the church as special people. The custom grew up that allowed these would-be martyrs to issue a ticket that would allow other Christians who had faltered to be forgiven and to be reconciled with the church. These martyrs were not ordained. They did not have any legal or official authority. But it was only on their authority that other Christians who had apostasized could be once again reconciled with the whole community of the church. There is even some evidence, that when they were at Eucharist, they were invited to preside —though they were not the ordinary presiders. Wherever the martyr appeared, his charismatic witness and presence was authority enough to allow that kind of leadership to exercise itself for the good of the community. In other words there was, in this period, a very ecclesial understanding of church authority, calling for full community participation with a strong centering of authority in leaders chosen by the community who already at that time were beginning to be recognized as "the overseer" or "bishop."

The year 311, with the Edict of Milan, marks a new era in the church. With Constantine the church became officially recognized. The clergy were given extraordinary privileges:

exemption from military service, and from being tried by civil courts. Bishops became nobles ranked with senators, and they shared in the administration of justice. They cooperated in defense preparations for the city. They really became representatives not only of the spiritual but also of the civic needs of their people. They became a class set apart in that new society because of the privileges and titles accorded by the law.

It was not only this legal recognition, but other things as well began to creep in to separate the ordained cleric more and more from the community. Celibacy was introduced and became one of the significant divisive factors because it meant that clergy now began to have not only a different function but a different lifestyle. From the fifth century on they were required to dress differently and to live differently and the separation of the leader, ruler, bishop and cleric from the people became more and more pronounced. In fact, it is in some sense as a protest against this separation that we find the movement of monasticism taking place within the church. Benedict in the West, and Basil and others in the East emphasized that it is not honors and privileges that constitute leadership but rather the minister's spirituality and commitment to the mission of Christ. There were repeated strong protests from the leaders of the monasteries about the growing secularization of the clergy and their thirst for authority in the political and secular sense. The monasteries became the place where holy leaders were formed, and a good many bishops were chosen by the people at that time from the monasteries, known and reputed for their holiness and saintliness.

The understanding of church as community, which we saw in the early New Testament and in the Age of the Martyrs, continued to have its influence. Augustine, for instance, would say that: "For you, I am bishop, but with you, I am Christian."[3] In other words, I share with you your life. I am one with you. In fact, it is from this century that the

---

[3]Migne, *Patrologia Latina*. 38, 1483 Sermo 340.

bishops and even one of the Popes, would make the statement that: "He who would be the head of all, should be chosen by all."[4] So, the process of choosing their leaders by the community continued in effect. So strong was this sense of community between Bishop and people, that still another directive from that period advised: "No bishop should be sent to those unwilling to accept him."[5] This is all part of the history and tradition of the church! Some of the things being called for today as means of reform, are very traditional and have a long history of presence in the church. Even as the process of secularization crept into the church, and began to separate the clergy from the people, this ability to have some say in the selection of their own leaders served to maintain some unity between leader and people.

It is with the beginning of the Middle Ages that we find a radical change in the understanding of leadership and authority. The reform of the church, begun by Pope Leo IX in 1054 — at the time of the East/West Schism and vigorously carried through by Gregory VII in 1081, marks the real turning point in the history of authority in the church. The major aim of these reforms was to liberate the church from the control of secular princes and other political figures, who were manipulating church offices and church property. The fact that this kind of reform was called for, confirms the power and presence of the laity in the church from the fourth to the eleventh centuries. In fact, it was an excessive power that led to manifold abuses that called for radical reform. Pope Gregory's vision of reform was aimed at making the church a completely autonomous and sovereign system, a kind of self-contained spiritual society that would control, not only its own people in spiritual matters, but also secular society. This vision is best expressed in the "two sword theory" that comes from that era — the spiritual sword that the Pope himself controls, and the secular sword that the secular state wields at the behest of the Pope. In

---

[4]This is St. Leo's formula in *Epist.* 10:4. (P.L. 54,628)

[5]Pope Celestine I in *Epist.* 4, c 5 (P.L. 50,434)

order to realize this vision, Pope Gregory ordered church scholars to collect every scrap of evidence that would support him in this vision of church. Thus, canon law was born. It was the monk, Gratian, who did much of this work and published his findings in what came to be known as Gratian's Decree. The collected evidence and selected events from early centuries presented the church as a completely autonomous and sovereign system, modeled on the Roman Empire with the kind of authority that was exercised by the secular leaders of that day.

It is also at this time that the term "Vicar of Christ" comes into being. It is a term that aptly crystallizes the understanding of church authority during this period. Although this term was used in previous centuries, it had an essentially sacramental or spiritual meaning. It was used to express the faith conviction that Christ and the saints work through this person. This sacramental image was now transformed to a largely juridical one, to signify the Pope as possessing powers given to him directly by Christ. Grace was no longer necessary in the person of authority. It was no longer important. It was not an essential for office. Simple episcopal authority, not moral authority, guaranteed jurisdiction and power. Never in the history of the church has the authority of prelates been so insisted on as in this period.

St. Bernard, reacting to this growing secularization of the authority in the church, made the remark to Pope Callistus II that "All this, as well as the claims to prestige and riches, goes back to Constantine and not to Peter."[6] It was not the understanding of authority that came down to us from the early church. St. Thomas too, in his theological writings, continued to maintain that authority in the church is invested in the whole congregation of the faithful, and not only in the office holder. His treatise, for instance, on the sacrament of confession illustrates this. There was a real struggle at that time in trying to assert that sacramental absolution is absolutely necessary for the forgiveness of sin.

[6]cf. Congar. *op. cit.* p. 142.

Thomas, however, continued to maintain that, although priestly absolution is important, in the absence of the priest one should confess his sins to a lay person. This was a practice common throughout the early Middle Ages, especially in the East, where the real spiritual leaders of the people were not the hierarchically appointed ones but the monks and the spiritual Fathers of the desert. They were the real leaders whom people turned to for direction, and whom they regarded as the holy ones.

Likewise in his commentary on Matthew 16 — about Peter and the rock and the keys — Thomas interprets this passage essentially as referring to Peter's confession of faith as the kind of faith that is to be the rock and foundation of the church. Such faith becomes a source of real authority, but not a source of domination and power. Thomas repeatedly insists that the new law is the law of the Spirit. It is a law of love and service — not a law of rules and domination — nor a law of fear and slavishness. In the theological world of the Middle Ages, especially that of St. Thomas, the historical understanding of church as community persisted as well as the concept of leadership as serving the proclamation of the Kingdom. But in many other areas of the church the efforts at reform were successful in transforming the authority into a legalistic, autonomous, secular understanding of authority as the power to control, to dominate,and to rule. It is not surprising that this insistence on authority in the secular sense led to the departure from the church of a great many Christians who had a different understanding of the authority, and eventually resulted in the Protestant Reformation.

The final historical section extends from the Council of Trent to the present day. The opposition of the reformers was not simply opposition to corrupt authority (which was quite prevalent in the late medieval period) , but opposition to authority as it was being exercised in the church. In response, the reformer asserted the basic freedom of the individual to be guided by Christ. The official church, on its part, continued to place more and more emphasis on the power and authority of the church. The Pope became the universal Bishop regulating everything. Ecclesiastical authority became increasingly centralized. People were asked to obey not on the basis of truth but the status of the legislator who called for conformity. The leader was not considered one inspired by the Spirit but one who had the power to rule and control. This whole movement culminated eventually in the definition of papal infallibility. Some theologians of this era went so far as to speak of "the real presence of Christ under pontifical species," that is, under the species of authority. "To be one with your Bishop was to be one with Christ." "When the church speaks Christ speaks." Many of those same phrases had an entirely different meaning in the earlier history of the church. But from the Middle Ages on, the sacramental meaning was gradually replaced by an authoritative and jurisdictional one. For many Catholics today, the oversimplified misconception continues. When the church speaks, Christ speaks. The exercise of authority in the modern Catholic Church continues to be one that is largely centered on the person of the papacy. Instead of being rooted in Christ, collegial, charismatic, service-oriented for the upbuilding of the community, it has become centered in the Vicar of Christ, authoritative, legalistic and oriented to the preservation of the institutional church.

Vatican II attempted a reaction to the over-centralization of authority in the church. From the very opening of the Council, especially in its long debate over the Constitution on the Church, the Bishops rejected the scheme that began with an understanding of the church as hierarchy. It insisted on first talking about the church as mystery, that is, the result of God's action, not human effort. Then it described the church as the whole People of God including not just Catholics but embracing in varying degrees every human being who does not explicitly reject God (cf. 14 in the Constitution on the Church). This understanding of church is a much clearer expression of the kind of mission Christ called his disciples to be about, and much closer to the understanding of the New Testament church than the vision that had developed from the Middle Ages.

Our understanding of church and its mission is intimately related to our understanding of church authority and how it ought to be expressed. In the Vatican II documents, there is a real trend towards recognizing and re-establishing the understanding of the church as the People of God. In many statements of Vatican II, the mission of the church is recognized as the responsibility, not only of the prophetic and teaching function, but the ruling and the sanctifying function as well. The call for greater collegiality throughout the church, from parish councils to national councils, is but one indication of this direction. The recognition by the Council that the Spirit is present in other Christian communities, and that authentic believers are those who respond, not out of conformity or blind obedience, but out of freedom, point to the real source of authority in the church. All these concepts flow from Vatican II's attempt to restore and recapture the early biblical and ecclesial notion of authority. By focusing in on some of the official statements of the church in the brief period before Vatican II, and then during Vatican II and after, we can telescope much of this history, and reflect on what has happened, and what is happening to the notion of authority. We will be focusing specifically on the teaching authority of the church, but similar observations can and should be made with regard to the administrative and sanctifying operations of the church. Vatican II's understanding of authority is most clearly expressed in the way the Council defines the teaching authority of the church.

It must come as a surprise to anyone who reflects on the church's history, that it took almost nineteen centuries for the church to come to a proclamation of papal infallibility. What that is saying is that for the greater part of nineteen centuries, the evolution and development of church doctrine did not depend primarily on official authoritative church proclamation for its acceptance. If your memory were to be challenged to recall the greatest contributors to developing church doctrine, names like Augustine, Tertullian, Thomas, Bonaventure and others are far more likely to surface than any of the popes. Insights were accepted because their presenters spoke with authority, that is, with convincing argumentation, and not because they came from some officially recognized source. Not only exceptional individuals, but the great monasteries and universities and many local councils and synods, made important contributions to the development and preservation of church teaching.

History reveals that genuine authority in the church was recognized as coming from many sources beyond the papacy and the hierarchy. It really wasn't until the latter part of the nineteenth century, largely at the insistence of the then pope, that the Council Fathers at Vatican I were ordered to focus their reflections on the power and the authority of the Vicar of Christ. It was this Council, to which there was considerable opposition (some American bishops and others left the Council even before it was completed in order not to have to vote),that made its declaration of the dogma of papal infallibility: "The Roman Pontiff when he speaks ex cathedra, that is, when in the discharge of his office as pastor and doctor of all Christians and by virtue of his supreme apostolic authority, he defines a doctrine regarding faith or morals to be held by the universal church, by the divine assistance promised to him by blessed Peter is possessed of that infallibility with which the Divine Redeemer willed that His church should be endowed for defining doctrine regarding faith or morals. And, therefore, such definitions of the Roman Pontiff are irreformable of themselves and not from the consent of the Church." When one analyzes the statement of the dogma, it becomes clear that the number of infallible statements that meet these requirements is truly minimal. The Council itself made it very clear that with regard to morality, the declaration really did not authorize the Pope to speak on concrete, specific, ethical issues with infallibility. They simply recognized that as impossible, because moral decisions and judgments in the concrete, must always consider particular circumstances, conditions and situations that are ever-changing.

And so, the doctrine of infallibility in the life of the ordinary Catholic, ought not be a major issue as it is expressed in the dogma. As it is popularly understood, however, and because of the way authority has been exercised, it has become a very controlling force that makes the Pope identical with Christ and every statement of the Pope or hierarchy practically unquestionable! Frequently, I receive a call that says: "Father, what does the church think about...? I don't want to know what theologians teach. I want to know what the church teaches!" A great many of our people identify the teaching of Christ in an absolute way with the teaching of the church. And they make that identification without reflection, without challenging, and without questioning, even when it is destructive to the mission of the church, and to themselves. This is not what the dogma calls for, but it is what too often constitutes the reality in the church. This unhealthy imposition of authority was nurtured in no small way by Pius XII in his encyclical *Humani Generis* (1950). Concerned about some of the developments especially in biblical theology that were raising disturbing questions about the creation story, original sin, and evolution and fearful for the faith of the people, he declared: "Nor must it be thought that what is expounded in Encyclical Letters does not of itself demand consent, since in writing such Letters the Popes do not exercise the supreme Power of their Teaching Authority. For these matters are taught with the ordinary teaching authority, of which it is true to say: "He who heareth you, heareth me," and generally what is expounded and inculcated in Encyclical Letters already for other reasons appertains to Catholic Doctrine. But if the supreme Pontiffs in their official documents purposely pass judgment on a matter up to that time under dispute, it is obvious that that matter, according to the mind and will of the same Pontiffs, cannot be any longer considered a question open to discussion among theologians."[7] The statement

---

[7]Pius XII. *Humani Generis*. 1950, Par. 20.

from Scripture, quoted here out of context, is used to justify an all too neat division between church leadership and laity. Such an understanding, as we have seen, was not part either of the New Testament or of the early church.

This statement of Pius XII was the final culmination of the attempt to center absolute authority in the person of the so-called Vicar of Christ. Not only were these matters of faith that were proposed in an infallible manner,but any judgment that the Pope would make a decision on can no longer be considered open to public debate or discussion in the church. This was an era, not too long ago, when many of our theological leaders were forced to resign their posts, or pursue their search for truth in silence. Teilhard de Chardin is just one of the better known casualties of that era.

At the Second Vatican Council called by John XXIII, the bishops at the very first session overwhelmingly rejected the statement of Pius XII from *Humani Generis* as an adequate expression of their understanding of the official church's teaching authority. It simply was not reflective of their understanding of the teaching authority of the church. In its place, after much dialogue and reflection, they substituted what is now paragraph 25 of the Constitution on the Church: "In matters of faith and morals, the bishops speak in the name of Christ and the faithful are to accept their teaching and adhere to it with a religious assent of soul. This religious submission of will and mind must be shown in a special way to the authentic teaching of the Roman Pontiff even when he is not speaking ex cathedra. That is, it must be shown in such a way that his supreme magisterium is acknowledged with reverence; the judgments made by him are sincerely adhered to according to his manifest mind and will. His mind and will may be known chiefly either from the character of the documents, from his frequent repetition of the same document, or from his manner of speaking." To the uninitiated, unfamiliar with theological language and history, this statement appears to be not much an improvement on *Humani Generis*. The practical conclusion that most people would draw would be that when the Pope speaks, one has no alternative but to accept and consent. A more precise and theological understanding of the terminology used, however, indicates a radical difference in the two statements (and the bishops were clearly aware of it). Vatican II uses the expression "religious assent" to describe the response Catholics are to give to non-infallible church teaching. This is a classical, long-standing theological expression to describe the kind of teaching that the faithful Christian has a right to dissent from and remain a good Catholic. Another expression "the assent of faith" was used to describe the understanding that the faithful must give to infallible church teaching. Actually, it would be a more faithful translation of the original Latin to speak of "religious respect" rather than "religious assent." The tradition of the church has always recognized the right to dissent from non-infallible teaching and this would not be possible if one were obliged to give assent. The Latin word used in the original text is "obsequium" which translates "respect." The bishops could have used the Latin word "assensum," meaning assent, but deliberately chose not to do so. To show religious respect for a teaching means to accord that teaching the presumption of truth, and to give it careful and prayerful consideration in forming one's convictions. If, however, such careful reflection reveals the statement to be inadequate or unconvincing, the right to withhold assent has always been recognized in church tradition. And so, the statement of Vatican II is significantly different from that which is found in *Humani Generis*. Vatican II acknowledges the freedom and responsibility to assent out of conviction and not simply on the basis of official authority.

Later in the Council the bishops realized that they needed to develop this topic more and to express themselves more clearly. One of the difficult issues troubling the church at that time was the sensitive issue of contraception. In the days before Vatican II, priests made the decision as to whether or not permission could be given to practice rhythm. To guide them in this decision they were taught to grant permission only "to those who have fulfilled their responsibility as regards the continuation of the human race. " In searching for a more precise answer as to when that responsibility is fulfilled, books of the 1940s and the 1950s would declare it required having six to eight children. The application of that rule was very simple and sometimes very destructive. Vatican II with its new appreciation of authority, rightfully took away that power from priests when it said: "Parents themselves, should ultimately make this judgment in the sight of God." Not the priest! Not the state! But the individuals, with the God-given freedom and right in conscience to make their own decisions about how to respond to God's invitation to be procreatively responsible.

The document goes on to say that in the matter of contraceptive means spouses should be aware that they cannot proceed arbitrarily. Obviously, it is not a question of whim or feeling. It needs to be a serious decision. The longest debate in the four years of Vatican II was triggered by a simple sentence which read: "They must always be governed according to a conscience duly conformed to the divine law itself, and should be submissive toward the church's teaching office which authentically interprets that law in the light of the Gospel."[8] Some of the Fathers suggested that the documents were getting to be rather wordy and unnecessary words should be deleted. They made the simple suggestion that three words should be deleted namely "and should be submissive." Put a parenthesis around these words and the document reads: "They must always be governed according to a conscience duly conformed to the divine law itself and toward the church's teaching office." The difference between the words "must always be conformed to the will of God" and "should be submissive toward the church's teaching office" is crucial. It means that our obligation to pursue God's will is always absolute; our obligation to obey church teaching is considerably less so. After two weeks of intense debate, the Council Fathers voted 2,414 to 113 that those words cannot be left out because they would lead to a "too

[8]Vatican II. *Constitution on the church in the Modern World*, par. 50.

restrictive" understanding of the church's teaching authority. It is important to understand this decision. If those
words were left out, it would mean: Do you want to know
what God is calling you to? Listen to the church! It would
canonize by conciliar decision the kind of attitude that we
have seen developing, that identifies the Vicar of Christ with
Christ. It would substitute the teaching of the official church
for Christ. The bishops, gathered together in Rome from all
over the world, did not wish to make that claim. We should
not! We dare not! It is not in keeping with either the longest
tradition in the church, nor even with the present official
teaching of the church.

I believe this is important because one of the pervasive
attitudes in the church at the present time is still the attitude
that maintains: "When the official church speaks, one must
comply and there is no other option!" That is not the attitude of the long tradition of the church nor of the New
Testament.

In the *Declaration on Religious Freedom,* the bishops
once again returned to this topic, and reflected their conviction that the Holy Spirit (the ultimate authority in the
church) acts in all of God's people and the official church
does not control that Spirit. This conviction led them to
remark that "In the formation of their consciences, the
Christian faithful ought carefully to attend to the sacred
doctrine of the church."[9] This final statement calling
Catholic Christians to "carefully attend to the doctrine of
the church" helps to clarify and confirm the meaning of their
earlier expressions "to give religious assent" and "should be
submissive." As committed Catholics, it compels us to recognize the importance of the teaching function within the
church. We need to be grateful for that blessing! I would be
willing to defend the double thesis: 1) that one of the most
positive formative influences in the world has been the
teaching office of the church, and 2) if there were not such a
teaching office, it would need to be formed to help us reach

[9]Vatican II: *Declaration on Religious Freedom,* par. 14

more responsible decisions in this complex world. My plea is not to deny the importance and rightful role of the magisterium, but to recognize its limitations, and especially to avoid what would be truly sacrilegious: the substitution of human authority for divine. The bishops recognized that danger in the *Constitution on the Church in the Modern World,* when they called lay people to the exercise of their rightful freedom: "Lay people should also know it is generally the function of the well-formed Christian conscience to see that divine law is inscribed in the life of the earthly city. From priests they may look for spiritual life and nourishment. But let a lay person not imagine that pastors are always such experts that to every problem which arises, however complicated, they can always give him a concrete solution, or even that such is their mission. Rather, enlightened by Christian wisdom and giving close attention to the teaching authority of the church, let the lay persons take on their own distinctive roles."[10] We see here an attempt to re-establish that kind of relationship between leadership and people that was so prominent in the early stages of the church and in many of the succeeding centuries. "Often enough the Christian view of things will itself suggest some specific solution to certain circumstances. Yet it happens rather frequently and legitimately so that in equal sincerity, some of the faithful will disagree with others on a given matter. Even against the intentions of their proponents, solutions proposed on one side or another may be easily confused by many people with the Gospel message. It's necessary for the people to remember that no one is allowed in the aforementioned situations to appropriate the church's authority for his opinion. They should all be willing to enlighten one another through honest discussion, preserving mutual charity and caring above all for the common good."[11]

[10]Vatican II. *church in the Modern World,* par. 43.

[11]*loc. cit.*

A short time after the Council, when *Humanae Vitae* was issued in 1968, episcopal groups throughout the world felt it necessary to translate that encyclical in a meaningful way for their people. Most hierarchies issued pastoral letters. The American Bishops did likewise. One of the important contributions of that pastoral letter is its renewed recognition of the lawful right to dissent that has always been part of the tradition of the church:

> There exist in the church a lawful freedom of inquiry and of thought and also general norms of licit dissent. This is particularly true in the area of legitimate theological speculation and research. When conclusions reached by such professional theological work prompt a scholar to dissent from non-infallible received teaching, the norms of licit dissent come into play. They require of him careful respect for the consciences of those who lack his special competence or opportunity for judicious investigation. These norms also require setting forth his dissent with propriety and with regard for the gravity of the matter and the deference due the authority which has pronounced on it.
>
> When there is question of theological dissent from non-infallible doctrine, we must recall that there is always a presumption in favor of the magisterium. Even non-infallible authentic doctrine, though it may admit of development or call for clarification or revision, remains binding and carries with it a moral certitude, especially when it is addressed to the universal church, without ambiguity, in response to urgent questions bound up with faith and crucial to morals. The expression of theological dissent from the magisterium is in order only if the reasons are serious and well-founded, if the manner of the dissent does not question or impugn the teaching authority of the church and is such as not to give scandal.[12]

---

[12]Pastoral letter of the American Hierarchy. November 15, 1968. "Human Life in Our Day."

It is another clear assertion on the part of the official church that it does not have the absolute authority that was given to Christ by God. It is an admission that church authority even at its highest level is not a substitute for Christ and for truth. It is our responsibility to continue that pursuit of truth, to recognize the freedom and responsibility to do so, and to affirm the right of people, at every level, to make responsible decisions with concern for the whole church. Vatican II and its views on authority certainly constituted a refreshing interlude between that era in the church when the key words for understanding authority were "hierarchy" and "magisterium," and the present time when the signs are increasingly clear that the present official leadership of the church does not share Vatican II's view of church authority.

A recent presentation by Cardinal Ratzinger to 230 American and Canadian bishops in Texas in February of 1984 documents the current official understanding of church authority. Although he recognizes that there is a tradition of dissent in the church, Ratzinger rather ridicules it when he says: personal dissent is also qualified by the fact that the person who dissents may do so for any number of reasons not all of them substantial. He may not have understood the statement. He may have misunderstood another statement which affects his understanding of this one. The causes of dissent in a person can even be of an entirely sentimental kind. He may after all not like his bishop anyway."[13] The explanations Ratzinger gives for dissent are obviously inadequate and superficial. The fact that dissent exists because official statements are not truthful, does not reflect contemporary scientific or theological scholarship, does not square with the experience and conscientious convictions of the faithful, is not even alluded to. It is a way of trying to dismiss by ridicule. Such an approach is neither respectful of persons nor of the kind of authority that Christ and the earlier apostles exercised when disagreements on issues were raised.

[13]cf. *Origins.* March 13, 1984.

Even more disturbing is Ratzinger's assertion that although the faithful have a right to dissent "such is not the case for the teacher. A person who teaches in the name of the church is taking what is basically a personal dissent and exaggerating its importance and its damage by propagating it... But the particularly great damage here is not simply that he teaches the dissent, but that he teaches it in the name of the church. It is odd that the people who have great misgivings about the right of the church to exist in any institutional form seem to have no problem with the contradiction implicit in teaching in a Catholic school, which after all is an institution, and can, it really seems to me, require that the person who dissents should not, precisely because he cannot, teach in the name of the church or even give that impression."[14] The assumption here is that dissent is always wrong and always false, and therefore it is always going to create damage. A second assumption is that the official church is always right, and therefore it is a contradiction to teach anything different from the official doctrine. Such assumptions come close to substituting the official church for Christ and the Spirit. The danger of such sweeping statements is that they have implications not only for theologians but for every one who is teaching in any way in the church. According to the new Code of Canon Law, anyone who teaches religion, on any level must, if they are going to, as Ratzinger says, have integrity and be faithful, do nothing more than simply teach precisely and exactly what the official magisterium teaches. They can do no more. Let me cite one little incident to indicate that this is not exaggeration or distortion. For the last year and a half, there has been an attempt on the part of the Archbishop of Washington to remove from his diocese *New Ways Ministry* headed by Father Nugent and Sr. Jeanine Gramick. Their crime is that in their ministry to the gay community they present a variety of theological views — including the official church teaching — but without openly stating their personal convictions.

[14] *Ibid.*

The archbishop is insisting that they must make explicitly clear that their own personal convictions coincide exactly with the teaching of the church. This understanding of authority imposed from outside rather than from inner conviction may well overflow into other areas of sanctification and ruling. This kind of authority was not claimed by Christ and manifested in the New Testament church and for many centuries following.

As Hans Küng observes: "The New Testament message gives no basis at all for ideas about the development of the church which play down or even domesticate the idea of the reign of Christ. It is extremely misleading to speak of the church as the 'continuing life of Christ' as a 'permanent incarnation.' In such views the church is identified with Christ so that Christ as Lord and head takes second place to his church, which pretends to be the Christ of the present in constantly new incarnation. Christ is thereby seen as having abdicated in favour of a church which has taken his place, and become his autonomous representative in everything, and so has gone a long way towards making him superfluous... This 'continuing Christ' has need of the original Christ only as a dead figure of the past. The truly 'continuing Christ' is, of course, the glorified Christ in the glory of His Father, who so far from having abdicated in favor of the church, has firmly established his reign over the church and the world by his resurrection, and will not abandon it until he hands it over to the Father at the end of the world (cf. Cor. 15:20-28)."[15]

[15]Küng, Hans. *The church.* pg. 310.

Reflections on the Present Situation

Vatican II called for a return to the original understanding of church authority, that is, Christ-centered, shared in community in a collegial way, committed to building up the community and exercised according to the principle of subsidiarity. The historical development, which viewed church authority as exclusively hierarchical, legalistic, autonomous and autocratic, the Council regarded as an inadequate representation of the true understanding of authority in the church. More recent developments, however, give the impression that there is once again a serious attempt, at the highest administrative levels, to reinforce the hierarchical, secular, legalistic understanding of church authority. Lest we fall prey to a narrow, personal, subjective judgment we need to read the signs of the times carefully, but I do believe that these signs taken cumulatively speak quite strongly. They result in more than just a suspicion or a feeling. It is a reality that is being experienced daily with increasing force in the church.

The first sign of this retrenchment was the calling of the Dutch Bishops to Rome to settle the differences in the Dutch church. Time does not permit us to go into all the details, but the fact that they were called to Rome (they did not initiate or invite themselves), and that a review committee with voting power was unquestionably stacked against them, is a good illustration of what is meant by secular authoriarianism. This sign was followed by several others: the authoritative intervention in the situation of the Jesuit community, the theological investigation into the writings of Hans Küng and Edward Schillebeeckx, and more recently by the imposed investigation of American seminaries. In all of these instances, the process was not initiated at the local level, but rather from the highest level, with little meaningful input from the level where the action really belongs. The Sacred Congregation's confrontation with the Mercy Sisters on the issue of sterilization, the imposed investigation into American religious life, and a number of provisions of the new Code of Canon Law further confirm this direction. The collegial structures introduced by Vatican II, which attempted to have authority become part of the living community of the church in all ecclesial structures from the parish synod to the national pastoral assembly, have been to a great extent ignored. Even the international Bishops' Synod no longer issues its own documents, as previously, but merely makes recommendations, on the basis of which the Holy Father presents his reflections of the Synod. The individual instances of Robert Drinan, Agnes Mansour, Bishops Hunthausen and Sullivan, the priests in the Nicaraguan Cabinet, Jeanine Gramick and Bob Nugent of *New Ways Ministry*, and most recently, the forced withdrawal of the imprimatur from Anthony Wilhelm's *Christ Among Us* and Philip Keane's work on human sexuality, reveal the breadth and depth of this current surge of repressive authority. Particularly frightening is the manner in which this control and repression is exercised by the church: without consultation, without due process or recourse, often in violation of its own procedures and with a secrecy that violates basic human rights and fundamental justice.

The Catholic Theological Society together with the Canon Law Society, have been working for the past several years on a document that would try to establish some means of resolving differences between the hierarchical authority and theologians. Their hope was to develop some forum or process by which these tensions and disagreements might be mediated. They have produced a fine proposal but to this date, it has not been agreed to by the American Bishops. Even should it be approved, it would probably have little effect. The official church often prefers to operate in these matters subtly, indirectly and secretly, rather than in a public open forum. Unacceptable theologians are disenfranchised by the institution more diplomatically. As an example, two of the most respected Catholic theologians here in the United States, Father Richard McCormick and Father Charles Curran, have the distinction of never having been appointed to serve on a Bishops' Committee. The rest of the world recognizes their authority. Their peers recognize that they speak with authority. Their opinions are respected, sought after and listened to because they are challenging, confronting, and enlightening. In official circles, however, in areas where decisions are being made and positions are being formulated, such voices are not to be heard.

What is the living church to do in a situation where the official authority that is exercised in the church, is really an authority of power, of domination, of control — a far cry from the biblical, traditional ideal that prevailed in much of the history of the church? I would like to present four proposals that attempt to respond to this dilemma. These proposals reflect the variety of responses open to the Christian community, as we go through what Karl Rahner calls "a dark, long winter of the church." In my own terminology I have labeled these four possible responses: the "personal," the "prophetic," the "pastoral," and the "ecclesial."

The first proposal is taken from an article by John Wright published in *Communio* in the winter of 1980 and entitled "Authority in the church Today: A Theological Reflection." He writes:

> The following practical suggestions arise from the previous reflections on authority in the church and from a consideration of our present situation. They are offered to all who find themselves affected by the tension in the

church surrounding authority, both to those who exercise authority and to those whom they serve through this exercise, though the application will be from somewhat different perspectives.

He makes six recommendations:

1. "In any situation of tension or conflict, try to grasp the insight and values of those who differ from you without attributing either stupidity or ill-will to them. Ask yourself how, what they legitimately affirm, can be reconciled with your own point of view and incorporated into it."

This is an appeal and an exhortation that is both honest and real and important and necessary. We really need to try to understand the reason behind the renewed emphasis on the authority to control. Does it result from fear of what pluralism can do to church unity? In 1976, *Time* magazine featured an issue entitled "U.S. Catholicism: A church Divided." In this article the writer commented on the great differences in the American church: whether the Mass should be in Latin or in the vernacular; whether the music should be Gregorian, guitar, or classical; whether there should be women or men priests; whether priests should be married or unmarried; widespread disagreement on the issues of contraception, sterilization, abortion, sexuality, and others. They pictured the American Catholic scene as a church torn asunder and divided. It is unfortunate that *Time* magazine, the secular press, and often our own people do not understand the church. Such differences on the issues mentioned are not a matter of faith. They are not issues that necessarily bind us as a community of faith, and they are issues where legitimate diversity is allowed and needs to be recognized and respected. A far more appropriate and correct title would have been: "U.S. Catholicism - A Church Diversified." The great fear that the unity of the church is threatened is one of the principal reasons why those in positions of authority are responding in so authoritarian a way. Unfortunately, this kind of unity, a unity of compulsion and imposition, is not the unity of faith and love that really ought to characterize the Christian community.

A second reason for this fear is the sudden serious drop in vocations following upon Vatican II. The recently ordered investigation of American seminaries and investigation of religious life, is an attempt to change and correct this pattern. If one looks at the pre-Vatican II model of the church, and regards ministry as the sole prerogative of ordained or consecrated people, then the future of the church according to present statistics is dismal indeed! If, however, one notices the kind of revitalization of the ministry of service that has been called forth by Vatican II, in terms of renewed religious, and more competent, prepared and dedicated laity, then one assesses the situation quite differently. If celibate, consecrated, and ordained vocations were continuing to come in large numbers in countries that barely experienced Vatican II (e.g. Poland), then there would be some basis for alleging that the trends of Vatican II have been responsible for the decline. The truth of the matter, however, is that vocations, even in so Catholic a country as Poland, are proportionately less numerous than they are here in the United States.

A third reason for the return to authoritarianism is that this will help eliminate the confusion and uncertainty following upon Vatican II. Again and again, in statements of the Holy Father and of people like Ratzinger, the right of the faithful to certitude, clarity and exactness about the truths of faith is emphasized. There is a real attempt to provide that kind of certitude and absoluteness. Erich Fromm once observed: "Many people today prefer the certitude of error to the ambiguity of reality." The certitude of the Christian, however, is not to be found in dogmatic pronouncements but in the awareness that our loving and caring God walks with us, and that life is a continuous adventure in grace. Life with our God and in God's world is never predictable. With Christ walking with us, however, we fear neither principalities nor powers, nor dominations nor death itself. Even though we can appreciate the concern of those who advocate a return to authoritarianism, such an approach will not solve the dilemma.

Wright's second recommendation is:

2. "In every written norm or regulation, especially one that creates a problem or difficulty, consider the goal or value that it is calculated to achieve. For this value is the basic ground of the obligation that the law induces or specifies. And it must always be achieved wherever possible. When this is done, the regulation has been substantially observed, even if some incidental failure is present."

What he is recommending is that we develop a healthy philosophy of law. We need to understand the limitation and imperfection of all law. St.Thomas observed that: "No law can be so perfect that it should never suffer an exception." Human circumstances and conditions are so varied and so different,that no law can be universally and absolutely valid. An old spiritual director in the seminary had a way of illustrating this truth. He maintained that he could never recommend for ordination a seminarian who never broke the rule. A priest who never missed his breviary, in his mind, could never have been a good priest. The law is meant to serve people and not people the law. It is this kind of understanding of law that we must be aware of when dealing with legal directives and regulations. At times, however, the very value that the law intends to enshrine may be in question. In such a case, no amount of *epikeia* or pastoral interpretation of the law, will rectify the situation. There comes a time when outmoded and outdated and destructive law needs to be reformulated and changed.

A third recommendation Wright makes is:

3. "Consider whether in a particular set of circumstances the literal observance of the norm as written injures some other value, especially one that a Christian would regard as superior. If it does, then the obligation imposed

directly by this other value, will require some modification in the norm as it is concretely applied. A literal interpretation of recent regulations concerning the role of women in the Liturgy (no altar servers, etc.) in some places could cause embarrassment, resentment, humiliation, and a diminished sense of human dignity in women."

Christians everywhere need to recognize the freedom and responsibility they have to pursue always the greater value. Christ is so clear: "The law is made for people not people for the law."

Fourthly, Wright says:

4. "Ask whether the failure to observe the law as written could cause confusion, scandal or bewilderment. Since the prevention of these is also a value, one must carefully attend to this in a situation where one might judge that he or she is otherwise free. For example, church authority may express public disapproval of certain theological or moral positions. You may have strong reasons to believe that the disapproval is too sweeping, but to voice support of those positions without the opportunity to explain and nuance could in some cases cause real scandal."

Situations like these recall Paul's words to some Corinthian Christians who were urging their knowledge as a basis for freedom to eat meat sacrificed to idols, although they were thereby leading some weaker brothers to violate their consciences. "Knowledge puffs up," Paul told them, "but love builds up." I think a counterpart to this in our own time is what we have seen in the recent Mercy decision on the sterilization issue.

Fifthly:

5. "Reflect that authority in the Church is rightly exercised to build it up as a community of faith, worship and love.

Laws which set more importance on the smooth running of the institution than on building up the community, on the external symbol rather than on the inner reality, or which are enforced simply to affirm authority, are alien to the nature of the church, and may verge on the tyrannical."

It is my suspicion that there are some aspects of the new legislation and of the present procedures in the church, that really fit this description of focusing on the maintenance of the institution rather than building up the community. Wright says: "Laws which do not ultimately deepen relationships of love and faith with God and one another, have no place among us. The warnings of Jesus and Peter to church Leaders are relevant here." This obviously is a recommendation addressed to lawmakers, but it is a recommendation that seems often to fall on deaf ears.

And finally, Wright says:

6. "Recognize that no commandment is higher than the two-fold commandment to love. Each person must decide before God how the values intended by law and proclaimed by the Gospel may best be achieved in these circumstances, always maintaining a presumption in favor of the law as written. Unity and peace are both fruits of the Holy Spirit more than effects of human striving."

One needs to recognize not only the freedom but the responsibility to follow one's reflected, considered, prayerful conviction. When people are asked in our own Archdiocese to wait two-and-a-half years to process an annulment before they can celebrate their intention of marriage in the church, I recall Paul VI's advice to the Curia that a delay of more than six months in reaching this kind of decision is a denial of justice. Justice delayed for so long, is justice denied. In such circumstances it is understandable when people follow the conviction that their right to marriage, in the church and before God, should not be restrained by the law.

A proper understanding of the official teaching in this area ought to encourage us to recognize both our freedom and our responsibility in situations of conflict to make our choice for the Gospel rather than for the law. For that is the real authority we are called to by Christ and by the tradition of the church. It may create tension within oneself and for others, but then we must know where our responsibility and our commitment lie.

I believe Wright's recommendations are important for the kind of personal attitudes that we must form, living in a church that presently creates tension between one's faith and love commitment to the Gospel and the authoritarian legislation of the church. One needs to develop, internalize and externalize that Christian freedom that Christ has given to us, and Paul so often emphasized.

A second possible response is the one which I termed "prophetic." This approach contrasts sharply with John Wright's exhortation to work quietly and indirectly to achieve the Gospel without being too disruptive. This type of response is best illustrated in a statement made by Sandra Schneiders in an issue of *Groundwork* where she speaks of prophetic actions in the present. She says:

> To be faithful in greeting the future is not to long patiently for a future we will never see. It is to bring about, here and now, a different present. And prophetic action begins with public grieving, the ceaseless indictment of evil structures and behavior, not so much by condemnation or blame but by lamentations. One can argue with an attack. One cannot argue with tears. Then, we like Jesus, secondly, must engage in the battle for language. What the religious establishment calls the divine plan for the complementarity of sexes, we must call sexism. What the political powers call strength and peace, we must call suicidal militarism. And only by calling the question by current definitions of reality will we empower people to imagine an alternative future. A

third recommendation is that we must announce a different order. Here and now, if we act out the equality of all
people by refusing to submit to, or enforce discrimina-
tory policies, they will be null and void. If we act out the
belief that peace is possible by our refusal to cooperate in
making war, and by our active offer of friendship to those
officially defined as enemies, war will cease. If we inaugu-
rate the true worship of God by refusing to believe in or
bow to the idols of religous power, and by preaching the
God of merciful forgiveness to those terrified by institutional threats, the oppressive power of so-called religion
will be broken. If we love, heal, forgive, empower and
liberate with every word and action, we will effectively
announce that the reign of God is here, now, among us.
Jesus did not do righteous deeds that no one else can
perform. He said: 'The one who believes in me will also do
the works that I do.' The reign of God is, in effect,
whatever Jesus' disciples are doing, wherever Jesus' disciples are doing his works."[1]

Those are fighting words! Very disturbing to an authoritarian structure. Lamentation, engaging in a battle for language; that is, exposing the honest truth of corruption and
oppression wherever it is, and announcing, in the sense of
living out, a new and different order, regardless of what the
declaration might be, is a very courageous stance. Thank
God that we have such people in our midst with courage and
strength; and they are many. The Mansours and the Berri-
gans, and yes, even some of our official leaders and bishops.
I found great hope in the kind of interventions that were
made by the bishops from around the world at the recent
Bishops' Synod of Reconciliation. Archbishop Vachon
speaking on the behalf of the Canadian Bishops Conference
about what reconciliation means today in the Canadian
Church said: "The Church needs to recognize our own

[1]*Groundwork*. May, 1984, p. 3.

cultural deformation, particularly the ravages of sexism and our own male appropriation of church institutions as well as numerous other aspects of Christian life. If we are serious about reconciliation, two steps need to be taken immediately: men and women need to learn to listen to each other; and secondly, we need to let ourselves be confronted by the Spirit." (Notice where he is placing the source of authority.) "We need to allow ourselves to be confronted by the Spirit of God in identifying those aspects of our institutions which are unjust and demeaning and in discovering what we must change to bring about the recognition of women as having the same full membership status as men."[2] To say that in the presence of the Pope and the assembly of the Bishops requires courage. To speak in the name of the Canadian Bishops conference requires great courage.

There were other similar interventions, but in the interest of time, permit me to share just one more. Archbishop Lorscheider from Brazil, speaking on behalf of its conference: "The greatest enemy of reconciliation in today's church is the spirit of domination. Is there a vice of domination in the church? Can it be affirmed with a clear conscience that discrimination on the basis of sex, color, social circumstances, language, nationality, religion, or race no longer exist among us in the church's bosom? The church goes ahead far better by means of dialogue and consensus than by authority."[3] I find that a courageous and strong statement. There were many other signs of hope coming from among those official leaders who spoke of an understanding and authority in the church similar to that found in the New Testament church and illuminated for us by the Second Vatican Council. There are prophetic people in the church, and they give great hope for the future.

The third and fourth response I have called "pastoral" and "ecclesial" — areas where problems continue to arise. In the midst of disturbing situations in these two responses it is

[2]*Origins.* Vol. 13. p. 334.
[3]*Origins.* Vol. 13, p. 357.

important for us as followers of Christ to recall the Master's own limitedness and finiteness. Christ did not and could not accomplish in so many instances things that seemed important and necessary for his dream. When he was asked to preach his message of salvation outside of Israel, he replied . . . that is not my mission. Sorry about that! He did not heal everyone who was brought to him. A number of times in the scriptures, crowds were waiting to be healed by him, and he disappeared from their midst. He did not convert or change everyone who entered into close relationship with him. Judas was, in that regard, a dismal failure. Christ knew very real limitations! And we too must be willing to acknowledge the limitations of a pilgrim church and to recognize that our decisions cannot always measure up to the purity of the ideal. At times, we must be pastoral and settle for the best that can be done in the concrete circumstances of the time and situation.

I have selected the four proposals or, in my own terminology, responses: the "personal," the "prophetic," the "pastoral," the "ecclesial," because they reveal the complexity and the multifacetedness of the problems we face in the present time. I believe that they all have a dimension of truth and ought to have a place in the total response to authority that must be our own. We need to be as clever as serpents in the gospel sense, and as simple as doves. If we examine the way Christ exercised authority, we will find parallels of how he responded to authority in each of these ways. He put an end to the harmful legalism of the Pharisees, not by asking for the destruction of the law, but for its fulfillment. He constantly reminded his listeners that law must serve people and not people the law. Christ could be "prophetic" and on many occasions he was. He confronted courageously the religious authorities of his day, revealing their emptiness and speaking the truth with authority. In a pastoral way, he responded by recognizing and admitting that the time was not right to go up to Jerusalem, or for his followers to proclaim him Messiah. Before Pilate and Herod he was silent. He did not heal everyone. He did not convert everyone. In one sense he could often be looked upon as a failure. We, too, need to be conscious of the limitations that reality sometimes imposes upon us, and to recognize that our call is simply to do the best we can. And, finally, in that ecclesial sense, which was the whole purpose for the authority Christ communicated to the church, he yearned and prayed that ultimately the pouring out of his life would help his people to become one. Ecclesial authority, properly understood and properly exercised, that is truly Christic, collegial, and service-oriented to the building up of a people bound together in truth and freedom — only that kind of authority will make that prayer come true.

Canonical Status

Emily George, RSM

There is in me and, I think, in many women religious, a
profound mourning about even writing of this issue, canonical status, that is ours today. For many of us, I think there is
a resonance about those lines of John of the woman who is
in labor because her time has come, yet who feels a new
surge of life when indeed, that child is born. It is obvious to
me, that something is happening in our lives. And so the
anguish that we experience, I suspect, should also be part of
that experience.

The large questions, for me, which revolve around the
issue are: What is religious life? For whom is religious life?
Or as Tom Clarke, S.J. who has been a great commentator
on religious life, puts it when he asks a very searing question:
"What is it time for in religious life?" His answer to that
question is : "Replacement — our replacement." Perhaps
that child to be born out of our anguish, out of life, will
bring something other than what we now do. I think we are
faced with the large question of what are we about. What is
our contemporary call? What is this vocation of ours, if you
will, in the church? Are we a charismatic, theological, ecclesial reality? Or, as *Lumen Gentium* says, "a gift of God
which the church has received from her Lord and which by

God's grace he always safeguards?" Are we a juridical ecclesiastical reality? Is there a conjoining of the two, and, if so,
how? Is it possible for the charism to exist without ecclesiastical authorization? Is it possible in the history of the church
that groups — men or women, have gathered as "religious"
but have not been favorably looked upon? It is not until the
twelfth century, I believe, that there was some kind of a
formalization about canonical status. What I am asking is
whether it is possible for groups to exist without official
church authorization and still have the charism we call
religious life. What comes to mind are the California IHMs
and their experience. Are they religious? Are those who
have specifically not sought canonical regulation, new
groups emerging in the church, who have missions such as
our own, are they religious? We are talking about something
fundamental — the charism.

When we talk about our life — what are we really talking
about? How can we capture it in words to make it intelligible
to ourselves and others? One way is to picture it as triangu-
lar in form. One side of the triangle has to do with our
mission: this group of women joined together in the Lord
prepared for the *mission* of the church. We know our mission as the experience of our ministries.

Another side of the triangle is what we might call *tradition*. Our tradition — what is it? Not what were the accretions that occurred over the years but the fundamental
tradition which the official, ecclesiastical church forced us
to look at as a result of Vatican II. What did we discover? I'd
like to put forth what I mean by tradition from examples of
my own congregation. I walked into a convent of Mercy
from one of the independent congregations not long ago
and on the entry to their generalate saw the document that
announced what I presume was the foundation of the Sisters
of Mercy. It said: founded in 1827 with the opening of
Baggot Street. Now the congregation wasn't officially
founded until 1831 when Catherine McAuley took her
vows. Somehow, however, 1827, which predated the official
canonical foundation is for us our beginning and we can

press it back to 1824 when the cornerstone was laid at Baggot Street; we can press it back to Coolock House where Catherine McAuley gathered the orphans about her and began to teach. Another example. We were called "the walking nuns" because we went out from the convent — that's part of the tradition — we went out! Those walking nuns! And we had a fourth vow from the beginning — contested over the years, canonically contested. It is the "service of the poor, sick, and uneducated." Sisters of Mercy make a great deal about the tradition. What I'm trying to say as we grapple with who we are is that we deal with tradition.

Mission and tradition make two sides of my imaginary triangle; the third is experience. Experience! What have been our formative influences? We can never be the same. I always tell this little anecdote from one of the bishops that I visited while I was provincial. I was visiting him about closing a hospital in his diocese and this particular bishop who served on the bishops' liaison committee to the LCWR said to me: "Sister Emily, you know where it went wrong for women religious?" I said, "No, Bishop, where did it go wrong?" He said: "When those sisters were educated. They no longer were docile." We need to look further at the experience of our ministry, a very troublesome canonical reality today because it touches on the emergence of women, particularly in our country. In 1963, John XXIII said in *Pacem in Terris* that one of three characteristic signs of the times was the emergence of women. And what about all those other experiences: the experience of 1965, at least when things were beginning to stir, and the experiences from 1980 to 1984.

If you take mission, and the tradition, and the experience, the question is: where does canonical status fit? In his book on ministry, Thomas O'Meara assigns "canonical rubrics" to a tertiary role. The issue of canonical regulations and status, needs to be relativized in terms of the basic realities of mission, tradition and experience. But there has to be, just by way of identification and service, boundaries to life. We have to know who we are, to whom we relate. Those are some of the tough and difficult questions, for groups that are choosing not to be canonical. Seeking canonical status says, "Yes, we want to be publicly identified with the church. We want to be authenticated, to be part of the public mission of the church."

My own congregation, the Sisters of Mercy of the Union, made a study called "Canonical Regulation of Women's Religious Congregations: Its Past and Its Future." We avoided the term "status" because that sends tremors through people. In the more practical order, it's not the status we're concerned about. Most of us, as I said, want to have the authentication of the church. We want to be publicly identified with the church. What about its regulation though? The genesis of this particular study, which was developing for a long time, came in 1977. We decided then that, as women religious in the church, we had to take an active role in our life. We developed what we called the Church Institute Committee to deal with questions of difficulty affecting our relations as a congregation to the church.

The minutes inaugurating the study raised preliminary questions: does canonical status add to the baptismal mandate? If the canonical mandate says we are more available to the church, what does it mean to be available? What church are we speaking about? What kind of identity does canonical status engender? Are there other models for establishing identity? What does canonical status mean to current members? In seeking answers to these questions, members of the committee were asked to do historical analyses and to consult with various persons who were not canonical, e.g. the California IHMs. We sought further answers to the following: What are the options to canonical status? What has been the experience of non-canonical communities? What has been the history of cloister in the church, and the development of the Sacred Congregation for Religious and Secular Institutes? What will be the effects of the new code on the canonical regulation of women religious? I might say that not a great deal has been done on this overall issue. Not a great deal, in fact, has been done on the history of women religious, partly, I suppose because officially we were not recognized until 1900.

The RSM study is basically an historical analysis, but it offers clues to the practical meaning of canonical regulation. We sought new understandings of canonical regulation as influenced by developments within the whole church, such as biblical renewal, the liturgical movement, and ecumenical efforts. We asked how the revised code of Canon Law also affects our current understanding of church regulation. And finally, we said: "Out of this reflection, let's work toward a conclusion. Just *toward*." That is what I am going to follow, and I'm going to insert, at what I think might be an appropriate time, the experience, the canonical experience, that we've had as a congregation that I think fits into the analysis of the issue.

Now for the history of canonical regulation of women religious. Between the second and fourth centuries, we see the emergence of the widows and the deaconesses within the church, the latter very active women as their very name indicated. Alongside this development, we also see the emergence of the virgins, the contemplatives of their time — some really free women in terms of their activities, but given much more to the reflective life than were the widows and the deaconesses. By the fifth century, the virgins were given dress by the bishops, the veil basically. The interplay then, in those early centuries between the active and contemplative dimensions as it affected women and their choices within the church was already evident. Between the fourth and the thirteenth centuries, we see the emergence of the monastic life, especially with Benedict. Women were very much part of this development. Some of the abbesses were very independent, had a high degree of self-government, including the governance in some instances, of orders of men. Many of the women's monasteries engaged in study, in nursing, and teaching: in other words, in an active life. It was truly an alternative lifestyle to marriage for women, legitimated by church hierarchy. In a recent issue of the *National Catholic Reporter* Rosemary Reuther addressed this period of history and these particular monastic women by saying they were in effect quasi-clerics. Their consecration was understood as membership in clerical office for almost half of the church's history. She said that from the second to the fourth century women continued to participate actively in pastoral ministry in distinct offices which received distinct consecrations, and were listed as part of the clergy in the early church constitutions. The role of these women clergy was directed primarily at ministry for women: such as preparing women for baptism, (escorting nude adult women into the baptistry), bringing the Eucharist to sick women, and counselling women, which was seen as perhaps unsuitable for men. Much of the personal ministry to women was in effect done by other women. Reuther's plea is that we should go back and claim our clerical roots rather than emphasize our lay status. Speaking of later monastic times Reuther said: Women abbesses continued to carry out a variety of clerical functions such as hearing confessions, giving faculties to priests to function in their territory, and distributing communion. Abbesses fit the title of deaconesses, and some wore miters to signify their episcopal status within their communities. But in subsequent centuries, the hierarchy sought to remove these elements of clerical rank from cloistered women at will.

The monastic movement not only brought about the kind of independence that Reuther and other historians would comment on, it also invited dependence among a large number of women. Some sought refuge in monasteries because they couldn't find a partner in marriage. And there is some interesting history about women bringing in a retinue of servants, slaves. Some of this kind of abuse came forward at the time of the Reformation. Some of the dependence was out of the control of women, particularly when they came under control of men's orders, and evolutionary loss as men's orders became clericalized, and as the papacy became centralized. By the twelfth century, Lateran

Councils (1123) forbade active apostolates for these women. In 1139, Lateran II imposed cloister for women. When we speak of it even now in our own times, we need to remember that cloister is not only a physical state of being but a state of mind as well.

The thirteenth and the sixteenth centuries are characterized by the rise of the mendicants, corresponding to the rise of the cities. Because of the inception of the second orders — Dominicans, Franciscans, Premonstratensians, and others — the mendicant revolution allowed some breathing space from the kind of monasticization that I've been speaking about. This provided women the opportunity to be true contemplatives, but they also came under the orders of men. In addition to the second orders the mendicants introduced the third orders of the Tertiaries, which provided for a dedicated active apostolate, such as we enjoy today. This, indeed, was a new way of being for "religious" women. Also, within this period of history the Beguines emerged. They lasted from 1215 to 1312, at which point they were condemned. This was a very interesting group of women, and also men (the Beghards), a response to the emergence of the cities. They were urban dwellers unattached to any existing order, and there was flexibility about their life. They could live alone, but more often they lived conventual life. They were characterized by poverty: they owned their property, but they could not use it. There was possibility of a temporary vocation. As long as they lived in convents, they promised celibacy. But they were free to leave and to marry. There was a certain stability embodied in obedience to local superiors and the diocesan bishop; they sought spiritual direction from the mendicants. Yet they lasted only a century. They ran into a lot of interference from diocesan clergy because they related to the mendicants for their spiritual development. Since they did not live cloistered lives, they were not seen as "true" religious and accordingly they were forced out of existence (although a remnant survives).

The period from the thirteenth to the sixteenth century was also a time of intense papal centralization. The person whose name is generally associated with that development is Benedict VIII. In 1298 (Periculoso) he mandated cloister and solemn vows for the universal church for both men and women religious. The end of the fifteenth century witnessed the decline of the traditional monastic orders of men and women and the rise of the pre-Reformation apostolic associations, such as the Oblates of Mary founded by Frances of Rome in 1425. The Oblates led a common life, were obedient to superiors, vowed poverty but retained the ownership of their property, and engaged in apostolic works. The church used the term "congregation" for the first time for this kind of association because the church needed a way to distinguish these women with simple vows from the members of the orders with solemn vows and cloister.

The period from the sixteenth to the seventeenth centuries is the period of the Reformation and the Counter-reformation. The Reformation not only challenged monastic decadence but also inaugurated a reform movement particularly among women themselves. Teresa of Avila exemplified this development. Along with this reform was the emergence of active religious, epitomized by the Jesuits and tried by women such as Angela Merici who in 1535 founded the Ursulines with a private vow of chastity, without a habit, with flexibility of lifestyle. Angela Merici also wrote the first rule by a woman for other women. However in 1612, Rome imposed solemn vows and cloister on the Ursulines. In 1609 Mary Ward founded the Institute of the Blessed Virgin Mary, the English Ladies, modeled after the Jesuits. Her associates had no habit, no choir, no cloister. It was suspended in 1631 and Mary Ward was put into prison. It was not until sometime about the turn of this century that Rome allowed the IBVMs to recognize Mary Ward as their founder. The Daughters of Charity in 1633 were established with the simple annual vows. This freed them from church regulation so that they could get on with service beyond the cloister. Finally mention should be made of the Visitation Order, founded as an active order during this period, but confined to the cloister by Rome.

As the result of Trent there is the re-imposition of cloister. In *Circa Pastorales* (1569) Pius V mandated that any group that did not submit to solemn vows and cloister could not take novices nor profess members. One could only leave the cloister in case of fire or contagious disease. Yet, let it be noted that at the same time, the official church was more anxious about regulating its women religious. There were numbers of men able to get on with the active ministry in spite of the universal application of cloister.

The eighteenth and nineteenth centuries represent a period of great ambivalence about who religious were, and where they ought to have been and how they ought to have been regulated. This is the period of the French Revolution, which had more to say about what we look like today than anything else; the period was also influenced by the vast migration of congregations across the globe.

To illustrate ambivalence of this time note the example of Benedict XIV who, in 1714 forbade bishops and the curial offices of the Vatican to dispense any member from cloister, yet in 1749 allowed diocesan bishops to approve active women's congregations to perform the works of mercy because they were badly needed by the bishops. The French Revolution brought about traumatic change on the scene. Because civil law forbade cloister, women continued to remain in the church, dedicated to God and willing to serve. What to do with them? The church recognized them as fact. These were some of the women who came to the United States. The United States bishops, on their part had countless immigrants on their hands and needed religious to live and serve among them. Historical exigencies had much to do about the canonical shape of religious life.

In 1864, Rome indicated that the United States bishops could recognize as religious, women who took simple vows and had a modified enclosure. And yet the Third Council of Baltimore of 1884, the council of the catechism, mandated strict enclosure for women. Strange things happened in that era — such as building bridges from convent to school, so the women did not have to go out into the world to get to their work!

Through the eighteenth-nineteenth centuries Rome indicated that the three vows were normative for both active and contemplative women, but religious status was accorded only to those who took solemn vows and observed strict cloister, even if the latter was civilly impossible, such as in France. Then, in 1889, Rome reaffirmed the religious character of congregations whose members lived the common life and wore a habit.

By the turn of the century active women religious were officially recognized as religious. In *Conditae a Christo,* Leo XIII stated: 1) that these groups would be recognized as canonical; 2) that there would be a distinction between groups having pontifical diocesan status. Because women religious had all too often been affected by the arbitrary decisions of their local bishops, they had petitioned Rome for surcease. The desire for Roman control, interestingly, came from the women themselves.

In 1908 the Congregation of Religious was established, which gave jurisidction over associations of both simple and solemn vows and over their internal and external affairs. The Congregation was further empowered to serve as a tribunal in disciplining cases, and to grant dispensations from vows. This Congregation was reorganized in 1967 into the Sacred Congregation for Religious and Secular Institutes (SCRIS), as we know it today. This period that we are talking about was also marked by the first codification of canon law which placed active women religious within the structure of the church.

What does this history tell us? First of all it indicates a tremendous impetus to adapt life to historical situations. There is the eruption of the charism over and over again, particularly for women. They started at one point, were forced into alien forms, but re-emerged later into fresh vibrant forms. The shape, the contour of these groups, often anticipated the times. We also witness the decay of old forms and their extinction. History also reveals both the recognition, that is the authentication of those charisms by the hierarchy, and then their taking control, at times very unfavorably. This process often was correlative with the socio-historical status of the hierarchical church itself. When the church was politically strong, it exerted greater control than when it was weak. A case in point is the French Revolution which forced women out of the cloister, and then forced the church to deal with these women as religious. The intensity of control has also been reflected in the prevailing theology of church and ministry. We see this in the "official" theology that came to the fore at the peak periods of the papacy. We see it reflected in sharp lines between the laity and clergy, a very important distinction when the church focuses on its hierarchical nature as one of its predominant concerns.

What I have just concluded was a sweep of history, and the clues it gives us of that dynamism called religious life. The first thing I noted was the eruption of the charism. This goes on, takes new shape and new forms, often because of factors outside of the charism, because of its history. I mentioned, for example, the French Revolution being one of those kinds of events that forced women out of the cloister, and then forced the church to deal with a whole new problem, to deal with the world outside and the prevailing anticlericalism. The history also gives us a clue in terms of law, church law, as it shapes relationships of the ecclesiastical church to its religious, whether that law is to coerce, to condemn, or to inspire. For example, there were canonical condemnations against virgins who committed sexual acts, very harsh prescriptive norms, condemnation laws that have come down to us through history. There were coercion laws about the breaking of cloister in certain historical circumstances, and how that was mandated. As to inspirational laws, when I read *Essential Elements,* the language suggests that the document is a guideline, which I would suggest is part of the inspirational movement, the kind of inspiration that we need as the motive force of law.

Another theme that runs throughout history is the prevailing notion of cloister which continues to linger with us not physically, but in the larger context of the psyche, of the reality of who we are, namely, that we need to be protected —protected from whom? But as we look at history, we do note positive sides to cloister. Women did need protection. Today, however, times have changed so that we wonder if cloister is to protect, or to isolate from the "secular," from the "world." There is also the inequality of imposition of cloister between men and women. Through the years that has been obvious and it lingers today.

Another theme that runs throughout history, and more fully than I can deal with today, is the bias against women in terms of jurisdiction. In the earlier times in the church, women did exercise jurisdiction; then followed the long period of entrenchment, so that Rosemary Reuther says, "Let's go back to the beginning." For us, I believe, that means the participation of women religious in determining their lives, participation in such things as being privy to canon law developments, where the decisions are made. There are restrictions we experience regarding the clerical dimensions of male religious, as they affect our lives as women religious, the kind of regulations, the kind of participation in the life of the church, the law, the bias.

So much for the early history. In the 1940s we come to new understandings as a church, of church life. We need to address church life as it affects the relationship of the hierarchy to religious congregations. During this period in the church at large, we note the great scriptural renewal (*Divine Afflante Spiritus,* 1943). In this movement of scriptural renewal, the IHMs were in the forefront. Also in this period we see the opening of our lives to modern critical methods: new sources; the challenge to the old; opening questions; the recognition of faith experiences; ecumenical efforts with a whole scriptural renewal. All have had a tremendous impact on how we look at canonical regulation today as it affects our lives. During these years we point to a great liturgical renewal, a more participative church, a return to sources. Not the least influential in the succession of events was the developing theologies of Vatican II, particularly the *Declaration on Religious Freedom*, that was really an American document — a disjunctive moment in the church, even though in order to promote it, John Courtney Murray had to say it was not disjunctive, knowing all the while, we were walking into a new day, a new reality in the church in relationship to other people, a church in a pluriform society. At the first Leadership Conference of Women Religious (1971) that I attended, the main speaker said that the church was for the world. I was really moved. That meant that we worked for this world.

Today, working for the world means that we give our best efforts to the ecumenical movement, a movement which embraces the whole world. It also means we look to ourselves, continue to use our combined energies to promote movements affecting women religious. We look back with pride on the Sister Formation Movement, a markedly progressive movement into the intellectual, spiritual realms; education in non-Catholic ecumenical settings. Who can measure what this pioneer movement has done for all of us, for the church? The documents of Vatican II were positive thrusts, *Perfectae Caritatis* and *Ecclesiae Sanctae* invited a return to the sources, suspension of accretions of the past, experimentation, inter-congregational cooperation, collaboration. The Leadership Conference of Women Religious (LCWR), the International Union of Superiors General (IUSG) federations are comparatively recent developments. In the light of the long history of the church, we forget how recent.

With regard to canonical regulation, canonical status, there are documents which have specific relevance to our lives, documents which raise questions for all of us: *The Code of 1983; Mutuae Relationis* 1978; *Religious Life and Human Promotion* 1982; *Redemptionis Donum* 1984; *Essential Elements.*

What do we learn about our status? When we read about the structure of the Church in terms of clergy and laity, we discover in that kind of division, as women religious we do not have a place; yet, we are hierarchically constituted as "a stable form of life" (canon 573). The structure between clergy and religious has a very deep cleavage. As women religious, we do not have a place in that sense. We are a voluntary association, and yet, as some commentators would tell us, in terms of canon law, there is greater church control than over the ordinary baptized Catholic. We know we *are* voluntary to a particular call from God that should make us free, yet the control is greater.

These documents raise another question — the treatment of women, women religious as women. We read about the papal retention of cloister for contemplatives, something about the participation of clerical, male religious in certain decision-making positions affecting religious, such as curial offices. Also we look at questions concerning the organizational model that is very important to us as congregations. I want to quote from *Mutuae Relationis* because I think it captures an important point. "Superiors fulfill their duty of service and leadership within the religious institute in conformity with its distinctive character. Their authority proceeds from the Spirit of the Lord through the sacred hierarchy which has granted canonical erection to the institute and authentically approved its specific mission." I am not contesting the statement. I am asking what it means.

Another aspect of these documents we need to address is the view of ministry, and for most of us, this may be the more central question. What does the document say about the source of our ministry? Is the source of our ministry our baptism or the hierarchy?

Given the tensions which may arise between women's congregations and church hierarchy, it is imperative that we work to identify obstacles to communication, use opportunities for collaboration. Zones of freedom for religious communities must be made more explicit. Procedures must be advanced to resolve interpretive disagreements and to mediate pluralistic theological views. Presently, there is no clear design in place for all of this.

Where then are we in examining the relationship between the institutional church and women's religious communities? Yesterday's reasons we find are not always applicable to religious communities of women since Vatican II. Past needs for group protection against secular and ecclesiastical interference are not easily translatable as present needs. Still the existence of groups as groups, within a larger church, is a phenomenon which cannot be ignored. The very visibility of these groups, their concerted efforts in ministry, their shared life — all make these communities of women visible to the whole world. Today what is determinative to each of these hundreds of groups of women religious is the call of a Christian community to actualize itself as community in relation to the larger church. The call is absolute. The acceptance of juridical status can only be for the sake of communion of life, growth in faith, service to the world, prophetic witness — Christian communities, all on the way to the Kingdom.

Canonical Status: Responder
Sharon Holland, I.H.M.
Canon Lawyer

Canonists have sometimes unintentionally offended persons who are seriously studying the question of canonical status, by appearing to make light of the topic. I believe their point is, that there are *many* forms of juridic recognition described in the canons. Besides institutes of consecrated life, which include all the diverse forms of religious and secular institutes, there are societies of apostolic life and myriad forms of both public and private associations of persons in the church. Given this variety of juridic forms, it is hard to imagine something which is truly "non" or "a" canonical.

The point of saying all this is that as new entities arise in the church — and they are arising throughout the world —they have many possibilities with regard to their identity

Sharon Holland, IHM, holds a Doctorate in Canon Law from the Gregorian University in Rome. She is presently an Assistant Professor of Canon Law at the Catholic University of America, Washington, D.C.; and is a consultant to various religious congregations. She served as consultant to the Papal Commission studying religious congregations in the U.S.

and form of juridic recognition. Since the Council, it has become familiar teaching that the gifts of the Spirit are given for the common good in the church. Similarly, from the earliest days, church leadership has been charged with the responsibility of authenticating new gifts as they arise within the community. The concrete details of how that authentication takes place have changed over the centuries. Much of the frustration and discontent of religious congregations today seems to lie in the complex and, at times confusing processes involved in maintaining the recognition of our giftedness and our ecclesial communion through revised constitutions. When a congregation begins to consider a change of canonical status, it must determine whether this is prompted by frustration, or by the actual recognition of a distinct new identity being prompted by the Spirit.

We are familiar with the story of St. Angela Merici in sixteenth century Italy. Angela intended something like today's secular institute, but within a few decades, many members had become strictly cloistered nuns. This is generally blamed on the influence of post-Tridentine bishops such as St. Charles Borromeo; but it is also true that members themselves did not fully understand or accept the intent of the foundress to establish something so entirely new. Today there are followers of St. Angela in every form of consecrated life: papal cloister, religious in apostolic works, and secular institutes. It is possible that some institutes today, religious or secular, have discovered that they were truly intended by the founder or foundress to be something other than what their present canonical status says they are.

I believe, however, that for many congregations of religious, founded for apostolic works in the 19th century, the problem is less likely to be one of mistaken identity which calls for a change of status. I believe it is more likely to be a struggle for a more distinct identity - a struggle for greater mutual understanding established across cultural, theological, and legal diversity.

I do not hear American religious saying that they no longer wish to be religious — although some have difficulty with certain aspects of current descriptions of religious life. More frequently what I hear expressed is a desire for greater understanding and self-determination. At the same time, when we accept that the church is a community or communion of persons and groups of persons, then we also accept that autonomy will always be modified by interdependence.

It may appear ironic to those who find this tension most painful; but institutes of consecrated life — religious and secular — have more canonically recognized autonomy than any entity in the church except for dioceses. By ecclesial recognition, these institutes become public juridic persons in the church — the canonical parallel of legal incorporation under civil law. As institutes of consecrated life, they each have "a rightful autonomy of life, especially of governance, by which they enjoy their own discipline in the church and have the power to preserve their own heritage intact. . . ." Local ordinaries are charged with a duty of safeguarding and protecting this autonomy (c. 586). No other organizations in the church have this kind of guarantee in the law as a result of their canonical status.

Because many institutes are still in the process of seeking approval of new constitutions, they do not yet feel the effect of this canonical protection. Further, there have been incidents which have caused serious concern about whether this autonomy will be universally respected. It is, however, the legal status of such institutes, and a change of status outside of this sphere would mean the loss of the legal guarantee. It is there, even if more time is needed for its more effective implementation and realization.

We have an analogy in our identification before civil law as a not-for-profit corporation. By this legal status, we have certain guarantees — certain exemptions from taxes. However, we also have certain obligations. We do not always agree with the way in which the law is interpreted and applied. Those of you who deal more directly with IRS (Internal Revenue Service) are very aware of this. We have learned to proceed very cautiously because if we violate certain aspects of the law, we lose the protections gained as a non-profit corporation. The implications of our actions have to be weighed very carefully.

Similarly, before a religious congregation proceeds very far in considering a change of canonical status, it has to consider the reasons, and implications. For example, a congregation may ask: "Did we discover that our founding charism, renewed in the spirit of Vatican II, really calls for an identity in the church essentially different from that which we have today? If so, what is it that we seek to become? If not, what is it that we really seek; and how can we best pursue it?"

Where an institute does, indeed, find cause to seek a change of canonical status, the process entered must include a thorough study of reasons and options. From a canonical point of view, the protection of rights will be of critical importance. We are very familiar with the formula of profession by which we vow our lives to God, "according to the Constitutions" of the congregation. Usually, our focus is not on that last phrase, despite its profound legal significance. The new law more clearly than the old, expresses not only the theological effect of the act of profession, but also its juridic effect. Through incorporation into an institute, the new member comes to possess all the rights, as well as the duties of a religious, according to the canons and the proper law, that is, constitutions and other norms.

Fundamental among these, is the right of a perpetually vowed member, given the parallel fulfillment of duties, to remain a member of the congregation for life. In an indirect but sweeping expression of the rights of individual religious, the canons, after a lengthy list of membership obligations, state: "An institute must furnish for its members all those things which are necessary according to the norm of the constitutions for achieving the purpose of their vocation"(c. 670). A congregation which considers a change of canonical status must keep a central focus on this obligation.

There is no developed process by which such a change

might take place. There is something of an analogy, however, in the processes developed for those congregations which have been forced to merge due to small numbers. No chapter, or governing body, or even majority vote of an institute, can simply decide on such a change and put it into effect. Every individual member must make a personal determination from the various options:

     a) to remain a member of the original institute;
     b) to transfer to another institute;
     c) to become a member of the new entity proposed;
     d) to request dispensation from vows.

If an institute, through on-going study, discussion and consultation moves toward a chapter discernment to formally consider a change, then a process would have to be established in collaboration with the Apostolic See from which juridic status has originally been received.

If, on the other hand, what is really sought is a greater experience of the institute's canonically recognized "rightful autonomy," there is no need to pursue such a process. Instead, we are returned to a study of the church's proper role in the authentication of charisms, and of the meaning and expression of ecclesial communion for religious institutes.

To this, I would like to add one further thought. It is the opinion of some, that something new is emerging in the church — some new form of apostolic life, which may or may not be identified as "religious" or as a "consecrated life." It remains to be seen whether the new will emerge from within existing institutes, or as a distinct entity. In the past, the church has seen apostolic institutes grow up as a sort of parallel on monasteries of purely contemplative life, taking from them some elements, but emerging as a distinct reality. More recently, secular institutes developed alongside of existing religious institutes; again, sharing some common elements, but having a unique identity. This adds to our ponderings whether today's religious are to become a distinct new reality; or perhaps are to foster and encourage new developments within the church, without changing our own identity radically. The answers to such questions emerge slowly, under the guidance of the Spirit. That guidance must take place, I believe, before we consider canonical adaptations.

Canonical Status: Responder

Alice Miller, I.H.M.

Associate Pastor

When I was first asked to give an opinion on canonical status, my reaction was, "canonical status, that is a problem for elected leaders to solve, a matter for others to decide." My work is parish work, not technical, legal, or hierarchical work.

However remote serious consideration seemed, incipient after-thought startled me with a question: "Suppose we lose or renounce canonical status and then a decision falls that bishops cannot hire us in the diocese. Where, then, does our ministry go?"

Upon more reflection, it came to my mind that somewhere in the history of the community, we sought canonical status because of the infringement of the bishop in our lives. Now we question canonical status because of the infringement of the Pope in our lives. Here was the reality that this is

Alice Miller, IHM, has a Masters of Education degree from Marygrove College in Detroit. For fourteen years she served as Pastoral Associate at St. Rene Goupil Parish in Sterling Heights, Michigan. She is presently associate pastor at St. Anne Parish, Warren, Michigan.

an issue for all of us; and I began to do some serious thinking, talking, listening.

These written reflections are simply personal, even somewhat extemporaneous. I have not done extensive research; I have no immediate answers, but I do have questions. I feel my concerns are shared with others within the community, and I hope that in noting these concerns, honest discussion will move us toward consensus in union with the Spirit of God and the spirit of Florent Gillet and Theresa Maxis.

Ministry is the focus of my life. Prayer, the community, the fun I have — all help me to be a better leader at St. Rene Parish. The fact that I am an IHM Sister, a member of a recognized group in the church, makes it possible for me to function as a pastoral associate in the parish. Could this be done, could I practice this ministry, in this way, if I did not belong to such a group? The answer is no.

By the same token, I am not blind to the injustice that exists in the ministry. I am fully aware of what could be and should be, and I know the suffering that comes from "having the game but not the name." Over and over I remind myself, as I make the priest look good at the altar and work to make the ceremonies and activities of the parish run smoothly, that it is not important who gets the credit. It is important that people are helped to be holy, and that the work of the church gets done.

We are living in a turbulent time when the sin of the church, in dealing with women religious, is flagrant. Yet, sin is not new in our church, and the challenge to overcome this sin is ours, but how? The very question breeds dichotomy, with pulling and tugging at both ends.

What would it mean to be non-canonical? How would it be possible to be an organization of the church, not recognized by church authority, and yet living and working entirely according to its rules and by-laws?

How might one become non-canonical? Could we, as a group, decide to become so and simply withdraw? Might we forget entirely, or fail to recognize the authority of the church — an authority we have needed and called on through the years, and now want to change? What sanction could the church bring if this happened? Aside from a possible rejection for employment, could our assets be taken? Would the very continuity of our structure be threatened? Who would handle community finances, and who would take care of our old? We have spent so much time and energy on our retirement fund these past years. Would it be easy to surrender it?

Sisters, I believe we must be open to the possibility of harsh retaliation from church leaders for any such action. Cases in point: the sanctioning of the IHM chapel in California when the sisters chose to disagree with the bishop; the showdown conflict over the public sector employment of Agnes Mary Mansour. This church will not accept a group of women, who for whatever reason, choose to go non-canonical.

Then, aside from hierarchical opinion, what of personal commitment and the promise we made to serve the church? So earnestly in our beginning days, we made a public profession of the evangelical counsels to Christ and to his church. How will we understand these vows in light of a non-canonical status? In re-reading *Perfectae Caritas*, that great document from Vatican II, it states again and again that it is through our vowed commitment that we have the call to serve the church in fidelity. How must we now fulfill this promise made so long ago?

Deeper examination clouds things yet more. As a pastoral minister, I have a problem with the word "church." Church for me is people. It is all of us — folks who struggle daily to live the Gospel and all that it means. It is those who work to put a meal on the table; those who worry about living in a nuclear society; those threatened by an age of robotics. It is human beings who party on Friday, join in worship on Sunday, and labor through the week to put that Gospel into daily life.

From that view, however, we cannot ignore the institutional church: the church of the Pope, most bishops, many priests, and all kinds of rules and regulations. This church is important by its great influence, and this is a facet that must be reckoned with. It is this institutional church that provides me with my ministry; and it is to this church that my vows are said .. hence, dilemma.

The questions are many and the current answers, none. We can only hope for understanding, especially concerning the meaning of obedience.

Looking back over history, it is clear that every age has had martyrs who emerged naturally, out of necessity, to stand up and make known the movement of the Spirit for that time. It was through obedience that persons or groups brought truth to triumph, and God's will was done.

The Jesuits have a long history of entanglement with church hierarchy. Often their attempts at persuasion met with some form of suppression, but finally the truth did win. The recent conflict with Arrupé and the choosing of a superior is but one modern example. The church is rich now with the writings of Teilhard De Chardin, but think back to his struggle and the cross he bore.

May we study and ask guidance of Catherine of Sienna and her struggle to be obedient to her God and to her church. She did not stand passively by during evil times, but directly challenged the actions of the Pope that were not gospel-oriented.

My stand is not for obedience without thought, without prayer, without the Cross. It cannot be an obedience of understanding that will enable us, the women religious, to live and work for the Church of the People. We are Mary Magdalenes who come to the grave and are told by the Lord, "Go, tell the brothers that I have risen and I am alive."

We sisters do not, as a community, jump on the band-wagon of change without considering long-term effects. Now is now, and what we face is John Paul II, CRIS, the Moral Majority, and conservatism. In time, these things will change, and what then of women religious which the church will always have? We must recognize and admit that we are living in a dark night of the church, a sinful, painful time.

But God is calling forth leadership to find the truth.

Women in all walks of life are called to this action; however, female leadership does not guarantee that change will come in peace and justice. The political guidance of Margaret Thatcher, Indira Gandhi, and Golda Meir have not always brought actions through peace. Our movement must be effective, but cannot be untrue to our beliefs. Rather, may we face our problem armed with knowledge and research; strengthened by prayer and fasting; seasoned by time and patience as we work toward a consensus.

We are daughters of the church. Let us never lose sight of this vision.

Canonical Status: Responder

Amata Miller, I.H.M.

Social Scientist

What can a social scientist contribute to corporate reflection on canonical status? First, it appears that the topic as we confront it today is really two-fold. We must deal with our response to the outrage we feel at the violence being done to women religious (and others) through the current administration of canonical regulations. And we must make our assessment of the advantages of canonical status as a congregation. It is my contention that we need to treat the two aspects of the topic separately.

Secondly, the perspective of the social scientist will focus on the life of the *group*, the congregation, in itself and in relation to other individuals and groups:

Amata Miller, IHM, holds a PhD. in Economics from the University of California at Berkeley. She is presently Coordinator of Material Resources for the Monroe IHM Congregation, and president of the Board of Directors for *Network*.

— the institutional church
— the people among whom we minister
— the societal structures of various types.

Thirdly, a social scientist approaches questions by gathering data, and so these reflections are based on

— reading of documents of non-canonical groups
— participation in one of the community days of a large non-canonical community
— interviews of some friends who have been or are part of non-canonical groups.

[Note: I am particularly indebted to Marie Egan, IHM, President of the Immaculate Heart Community of Los Angeles, California for her sharing of her reflections with me.]
In what follows these three elements of the approach of a social scientist will be woven together.

It seems to me that it is important that we look at the question of canonical status in terms of what it means to us as a group. As a congregation we called for this process of corporate renewal out of a recognition that as we came to full maturity in our individual renewal we sensed that we wanted to understand better the meaning of that group, that community in which we had all vowed our lives to God and to one another. We wanted to explore together the meaning of corporateness, the power of corporateness—in terms of our ministry, in terms of our life, in terms of our role in society, in our world, and in the church.

So, from this perspective it is important to do what the Sisters of Mercy have done, in their very pain, that is consider the reality of canonical status, official recognition by the church, as it affects the life of the whole congregation, and as distinct from the revulsion we have at the way canonical regulation is being exercised at this time. As Emily has pointed out, there is a variety of responses —one of which may be to change status. We need to ask what the appropriate response is in the light of our IHM life and mission and identify the trade-offs involved in choosing each type of response.

We must continue to search out the meaning of *group*. The question we are dealing with here today raised one that keeps cropping up over and over again as we confront different issues in our life together, and as our society experiences key dilemmas. That question is very basic, and has profound ramifications: "Is a group merely a collection of individuals, or is there something new in the life of a group? Is there a synergy that happens that makes the group more than the sum of its parts?" And if so, how do you make it happen that the group can be effective, more than just the sum of the individuals, however powerful they may be singly? Is the group life merely a support for individual life, or does the group itself have some reality? And if so, how do you make that group life vital?

It is my sense that it is part of our IHM corporate experience that the group does have some reality. We are trying to grapple with the meaning of that reality now, at this time in our history. It obviously means something different for us to be in community together now, than it did when we all went in lock-step to berry patches and to meals and to chapel and to bed. It seems to me one of the exciting things is that we are confronting this question in our arenas as a congregation in solidarity with so many other groups as society shifts to the right. The question which confronts us at the deepest level is: will we fragment groups and dissipate the power of groups in the name of short-sighted individualism, or will we learn what human community means in terms of the deepest values we hold?

It is incumbent on us in this search to identify the constitutive elements of the life of a group and to see how in our own IHM mission, tradition, experience canonical status— official church recognition— is a part of our corporate life. There are certain basic characteristics of the life of any group. Examining them in the light of the question of canonical status can be helpful.

First, a group has a distinct reality and visibility flowing out of its shared purpose. So we need to ask: To what extent is our corporate history and our experience of our mission related to the juridical status that we have had and continue to have in the church? Sister Emily pointed out that Mother McAuley's idea was that if she wanted people to join her, if she wanted her ministry to be acceptable to the people of God, there was something about the authentication that came from approbation that was important. It struck me as I was reflecting on our increasing mobility in mission, that there is something we take for granted, and that is that the canonical status we have — with all the pain that surrounds it — does mean that we can go literally anywhere in the world and do our ministry because there is a validity, and authentication, that comes from being able to say who we are, that is recognized by people and governments everywhere. One of the groups which changed to non-canonical status found that people kept asking them "Why did you leave the church?" This, along with ecclesiastical prohibition, limited their opportunity for ministry in areas where they had long worked. So, the question of canonical status raises the issue of the extent to which the willingness of others to join with us in ministry, or to allow us to minister among them is related to the public authenticity tied to this status.

Second, one of the things that holds a group together is a common philosophy and a common vision. When I asked a leader of a group which had changed to non-canonical status what a community needs to think about in considering such a change, she responded that a congregation needs to consider very carefully the vision of all of the members, to make sure that it is deeply discerned with everyone in the group. And so we would need to face the degree to which our shared vision is bound up with the official recognition of the church.

Third, flowing out of the common purpose and common philosophy of a group are the identity-sustaining processes and events. Every group has certain rituals and myths and place connections which express and form a part of its identity. Among groups that have changed status one of the continuing problems is that of identity. The members who were part of the change have the old memories and myths and "battle scars," but the integration of new members is continually difficult. So, the question of the extent to which our identity is tied into the place we have had in the church, the official church, would be one around which discernment would be needed. We need to recognize that for some of us more than for others, depending on our experience, identity as a group is somehow related to the official status of the congregation in the church. This status has been part of our recognized place, of who we are for the lifetime of all of us. When a community changes its status, it must discern all over again, "Who are we?", "Who are we going to be?"

Fourth, a group seeks stability over time. One of the positive elements of canonical status is that it connects the group to the whole tradition of religious life in the church over the centuries—with all the light and dark that Emily's presentation revealed. Stability, in a context of meaning which undergirds the group during various successive leaders, is critical to the continuity of purpose of a group — as various negative examples from the history of nations amply demonstrate. A group needs to reflect on how it would maintain those stabilizing elements, that continuity, if a change to non-canonical status were made.

It seems to me, then, that we need to look carefully at those questions which Emily suggested. What is there about our IHM tradition, mission, experience that would be altered by a change of status, and how? Or, putting it another way: What does the official status that we now enjoy and have enjoyed for many years mean for the life of this group. We have to go back to the very beginnings in *No Greater Service* to get the full look. How important is it? Therefore, what would be the trade-offs, the gains and losses that we would sustain from a change of status? What would we be accomplishing, and what would we be losing? How would we measure these two against one another?

As in most painful decisions of life, we are talking about values in tension here. Very clearly there are values on both sides. The first value of being non-canonical is that very attractive one of self-determination. As one member of a non-canonical group put it, "It's very nice to have that breathing space." That value is in tension with the values of external legitimacy, public authentication which gives a freedom and mobility for mission.

Secondly, non-canonical status gives more scope for spontaneity, flexibility and creativity. On the other side are the values of stability and longevity for continuity in mission. All important values.

Thirdly, there is the value of group autonomy—being able to set our own course as a group. In tension with that value is one intended value of canonical status—the protection of the individual from the tyranny of the group, and one group from other groups in the church. One of the particular pains of the present moment is the inability of congregations to rely on these canonical safeguards to protect their members from Roman interventions.

Fourthly, the value of independence, of being free-standing, is in tension with the value of being linked in to an organized structure which can have power. What we are conscious of now is the abuse of power within the structures. But I keep dreaming as a social scientist of what could be, if we could only have all the power of the institutional church really focused on justice and peace. People outside our Church look at us and say, "If we only had the organizational structures that you have, there is nothing we couldn't do!" So in my dreaming moments I think it has to be possible to create a way of collaboration which will bring all the power together in a way that really can minister to achieving the goals that we share in terms of a better world for all God's people, instead of having it tear us apart. If we can learn it in religious congregations and within our church, then maybe, just maybe, we can learn it in our nation and in our world.

As Emily said, we see over and over in history the tremendous surge of life that keeps erupting. I am certain that in our discussions of this question of canonical status there will be many eruptions of energy; and I am confident that together we will discern our place in regard to this question and we will move forward to discover our corporate charism anew.

Canonical Status: Responder

Mary Ellen Sheehan, I.H.M.
Theologian

Experience and law co-relate in a dynamic, interdependent way. Purposeful and effective law both arises out of human experience, and also serves to illuminate and direct human experience, especially with regard to a greater realization of the common good. United States federal civil rights legislation in the 1960s is perhaps a good example of this dynamic. The 1776 Declaration that all men are created free and equal arose originally as a protest against a society where human beings were oppressed and persecuted because of social status, economic conditions, or religious beliefs. Paradoxically, while the U.S. Constitution righted some wrongs, it took another two hundred years for this founding principle to return to experience, to haunt it, and force it to yield up more of its truth. And still today the process goes on, especially with regard to women and the

---

Mary Ellen Sheehan, IHM, received her Doctorate of Sacred Theology at the Catholic University of Louvain, Belgium. She is presently an assistant professor of Systematic and Pastoral Theology at the University of St. Michael College School of Theology, Toronto School of Theology.

poor, who in large masses are still treated as if they were unfree and unequal.

Similarly, theology as faith seeking understanding, is also responsive to human experience; just as human experience in turn is subject to critique from the prophetic function of theology. When law or theology becomes separated from the exigencies of human experience taken dynamically, each is liable to become oppressive, legalistic, or a deadly rationalistic system. Correspondingly, when human experience seeks total autonomy, it risks severing its natural orientation to community and religiously inspired transformation.

Experience, law, and theology are thus necessarily interrelated, and truth lies in the complex act of interpretation. While the history of law and theology shows that this has always been the case, our age is marked by a peculiar sensitivity to this process. Rapid and extensive change marks every dimension of contemporary human experience, with the added feature of our almost immediate awareness of this pervasive upheaval through inter-terrestrial and extra-terrestrial communication.

Theology, as faith seeking understanding in today's world, is actively engaged in a process of critique, retrieval, and reinterpretation. It is thus natural and normal to expect problems and tensions in the set of interpretation, particularly in regard to the law of the church, as it attempts to perform its function in the contemporary world.

The Revised Code of Canon Law itself reflects differing theological assumptions. Thus, more often than not, the truth and power of the law to promote the rights and responsibilities of the church's members will be known only in the act of interpreting the law. Thus, much is at stake, depending on the operative theology at work in interpretation.

Several shifts or transformations occurring in contemporary theological reinterpretation serve to illustrate this tension. Without referring to the specific sources of these shifts in recent theological development, let me indicate some of the major ones. There is first the struggle to reformulate the relationship between the sacred and the secular. Whereas in our more recent past, the sacred and the secular were viewed largely as an "over-and-against" relationship, current theological reflection focuses on the secular as the locus of God's self-manifestation. The church is no longer only "over-and-against" the world, but *of* and *in* the world and *for* the world. Consider the implications thus in the current Code for such key words as "witness," "cloister," "religious." While "witness" once meant being set apart as striking examples of evangelical life, today it may also mean martyrdom (its original evangelical meaning) in pursuing justice in the world. Similarly, with the development of baptism as orientation to committed discipleship, the word "religious" also becomes more extensive than it was at one time in the church. Religious can no longer be associated exclusively with being "set apart"; the word must also be able to mean being *in* and *of* and *for* the world.

Another shift concerns the conception of the church. Not too long ago we thought of the church as the perfect society; today we acknowledge more fully the historical character of the church as the pilgrim people of God, as a society "semper reformanda." Truthfulness in this new or, more accurately, rediscovered perspective admits to change, growth, development, even imperfect formulations. Thus, the law of the church also cannot expect to be in exact correspondence with either theology or the human experience it seeks to direct or clarify. The law will have to be interpreted in order to achieve its end of protecting individual rights and promoting the common good. It can no longer simply be applied unambiguously, if the always-reformable character of the church is to be recognized.

There is thirdly the factor of ecumenism as the context of faith and action in today's world. Church has self-consciously oriented itself in Vatican II to a process of ecumenical dialogue. From once proclaiming that it was the sole guarantee of salvation, the church has moved to a view of universal salvation. To be sure, the Roman Catholic Church keeps its own identity in this shift. But by reason of its new (or rediscovered) accent on openness to other Christian and world religions, its own formulation of doctrine, law, and church order will necessarily undergo change. In some instances, the reformulation of canon law and church order has not yet succeeded in being more in keeping with broadened theological development.

A fourth shift regards the transformation regarding spirituality and holiness. Where once the church stressed a hierarchical ordering of holiness in terms of "states of perfection" as greater or higher than "lay" holiness, it is now accenting the gospel basis of a universal call to holiness for all its members. All are called to conversion and the faithful following of Jesus in committed action for the manifestation of God's reign of justice and love in this world. Baptism is a call and mandate to ministry.

Whether intended or not by the framers of the Second Vatican Ecumenical Council, this accent brings new pressures to bear on the traditional lay-cleric distinction and thus on consecrated religious life which is "both/and" in regard to this distinction. Religious women especially are affected by these developments since they are not clerical (and thus lay); but at the same time have a more defined identity in church order than lay Christians. "Ecclesial women" or "women of the church" were terms often used of consecrated religious women in the 1950s and 1960s. But today it could be argued that many other women (and men) can be said to be "ecclesial." In fact, all Christians are "ecclesial" by reason of their baptismal call to holiness and its expression in ministry.

This shift raises up many new issues both for the formulation of church law and for its interpretation. What is distinctly different about these various groupings in the church? Is there a different morality or church law when *all* members of the church have the same basic call of fidelity to the church? How are consecrated religious women (and some men) lay? How are lay persons religious?

A current experience that illustrates some of these questions is the situation of the former Agnes Mary Mansour,

R.S.M. who was told by Vatican authority that she could not hold a public office that had responsibility for dispensing funds for abortions, in part at least because of the public character of her consecration to the church. Abstracting from the many other problems of interpretation in this recent tragic event in the church, one can in this regard ask why the same action would not be demanded of any lay Catholic holding a similar office. Is the church's teaching on abortion more binding on some members than others? Here might be a footnote on a recent case in which a child was expelled from Catholic grade school because she thought abortion was permissible. (Not by Rome, however, but by pastor.)

Another shift related to the issue of the universal call to holiness occurs around the church's current theology of its saving action. Basing itself on Vatican II, the contemporary church has aggressively and outspokenly pursued its call to proclaim the evangelical commitment to peace and justice in the present world. This active and courageous proclamation has shifted interpretations of eschatology and saving action from a relatively narrow cult focus to a more inclusive prophetic and transformative notion of sacrament at work in the world, challenging oppressive and manipulative actions against the poor and defenseless ones of our earth. In current theological development (as in earlier ages, too), this option for the poor is seen as constitutive of the Gospel, a duty, if you will, of faith from which no Christian is exempt. While admittedly there are complex issues in today's world, the church has committed itself (its members) anew to this evangelical conviction. Its formulation of law thus cannot be so simple or so univocally applied as to remove itself (or its members) from this complexity, as the recent events around Fernando Cardenal of Nicaragua seem to suggest.

A final shift is occurring in the area of power and authority. There is plenty of evidence in Vatican II theological reflection that the contemporary church intends to move from a more narrowly conceived notion of authority, applied simply and univocally in a hierarchical way to a broader, more evangelically based notion that includes participation, co-determination, and co-responsible governance. The theological foundations for this shift include the recovery of the Christological notion of authority as service rather than status, and of adult moral life as responsible freedom rather than passive acceptance. But a church whose patterns of the exercise of authority have been for so many centuries patriarchal and clerical is finding it difficult to reformulate its massive structures to be more in line with authority as participative and co-responsible.

These tensions will remain for some time, it appears, from recent events involving the Vatican and many local churches throughout the world. *The Revised Code of Canon Law* has reflected some shift, but it is yet a long way from guaranteeing the rights of an active, participative, and co-responsible model of church governance. At the heart of this continuing tension will be an increasingly conscientized laity, and in particular women, who by definition are excluded from any real authority in the church. Thus, women's religious communities which continue to engage in transforming their own internal structures and constitutions toward participative and co-responsible government, and similarly local church in their diocesan and parochial structure transformations, will continue to encounter resistance, misunderstanding, and injustice wherever the former model is still strongly in place. But this creative conflict will and must continue for the good of the church as a whole.

By way of summary, the following general conclusions may be made. First, these and several other theological transformations constitute the character of church life today. There is still a groaning toward the truth today, but the groaning is well directed by inspiration of the Holy Spirit through the Second Vatican Council. Secondly, in the face of the complexity of today's church and world in transformation, there is evidence of a tendency to pull back fearfully from some segments of the church and to rush ahead uncritically from other segments. This is the given context in which church law exists. No part of canon law in today's church will be employed easily, simply, and without questioning. In fact, the meaning of the law will only be established concretely through interpretation.

Thirdly, the church is still woefully behind in devising appropriate processes to guarantee rich and liberative interpretation which is the true purpose of the law. These processes must include right and full representation of all parties involved on an equal footing. If not, a certain mockery of justice will sow even deeper seeds of discontent and dissatisfaction. This is in fact the wide scope of power and responsibility that canon law and its interpreters presently hold. It is not an easy calling, but it is vital to the good of the church as a whole.

Fourthly, perhaps the greatest challenge of the church today, and for some time to come, is its need to transform itself from domination patterns, unfortunately associated with clericalism, patriarchy and sexism. These notions are not identical in meaning. They are not synonymous. But as long as authority can be vested only in ordained ministers (male clerics) arranged exclusively in a hierarchical fashion (thus patriarchal), all women and some men are excluded (sexism against both sexes). This form of domination no longer has viability as any thinking and feeling Christian knows. How all the members of the church go about this necessary transformation together in the name of Jesus is the real task at hand. One thing is certain; it is underway.

Section Two
Congregational Leaders Speak

Anna Marie Grix, I.H.M.

(1954-1966)

Margaret Brennan, I.H.M.

(1966-1976)

Mary Kinney, I.H.M.

(1976-1982)

Carol Quigley, I.H.M.

(1982-   )

Celebration

The date was November 10, 1984; the place, Saint Mary Auditorium, Monroe, Michigan; the occasion, a great homecoming to commemorate the founding of the Immaculate Heart of Mary Congregation, and to listen to the reflections of our four living general superiors whose administrations cover a span of thirty years. The Sisters assembled in Monroe, plus the many who joined them via teleconferencing from other parts of the country — some 700 women — represented not only a single community in a single city, but a microcosm of women religious throughout the country who are about the task of clarifying their own reason for being, re-expressing their common vision, re-choosing membership in their corporate body, and in a way, re-discovering their own congregation.

Leadership

A leader remains one of God's greatest gifts to a congregation, a changing changeless bequest. The 1845 image of Mother Theresa Maxis, the first IHM general superior, may seem to bear only small resemblance to the Vatican II concept of leadership with its emphasis on servant leader.

But the fullness of leadership has always included a calling forth the gifts of others, a pointing of the way, an invitation to transcend the immediate boundaries of time and walk into the unknown. Standing first among equals, every real leader "stays close to the customers," molds and is molded by the experiences of her time, learns to see in the dark, to risk, to trust.

As we begin our 140th year, the Sisters, Servants of the Immaculate Heart of Mary of Monroe honor their long line of leaders all through the years, from the pilgrim paths of Mother Theresa Maxis down to the four living leaders who have guided us during the past thirty years. On this day of thanksgiving even as we honor our own leaders, we salute women religious everywhere whose gift of leadership has enriched not only their own communities but prodigiously blessed the church and the entire world.

"All Down the Years..."
Anna Marie Grix, I.H.M.
(1954-1966)

It is a privilege to share this Founder's Day program with you. The invitation suggested we center our words around two questions: What did you think the future of the congregation would be when you took office? How do you see the future now? Please remember I took office in 1954. Thirty years ago. Since then, how much has come to pass everywhere in the world. At this point in time my best claim to fame is that I now rank number 49 in our community of 986, and my years of lived experience are 64. I decided therefore to share with you my best possession — my experience. To do that I propose to give you a panoramic view of IHM life up to 1954.

In 1845 Father Louis Florent Gillet, a young Redemptorist priest, a missionary newly arrived from Belgium, faced the problem of providing a school and teachers for the girls of Monroe. It was truly the Providence of God that led him to three waiting, dedicated women: Theresa Maxis, Charlotte Shaaf, and Theresa Renauld, eager to serve God and willing and able to teach. Our congregation was born in response to the needs of the time; and for 139 years the congregation has been responding to the needs of the time in its efforts to spread the Kingdom. On this day of celebration it is fitting that we pause with reverence, remembering in a special way those first pioneers and all our predecessors "dwelling now in light yet ever near", on whose shoulders we stand, and without whom there would be no cause for celebration.

We can only guess what each of the first superiors thought the future of the congregation would be when she took office. We do know that when our founder, Father Gillet, then a Cistercian monk, was re-introduced to the community he had been forced to leave thirty-four years before, he was amazed and grateful to God that the congregation had flourished. From his monastery he wrote that in 1845 he "began without thinking of the future of the work — leaving it to God to bless it and make it prosper if it were pleasing to him and useful for the salvation of souls."

In our congregational history, *No Greater Service*, we read about some of the travails of the struggling community during the first half-century of its existence: the devastation caused by the sudden departure of Father Gillet, the periods of spiritual desolation and deprivation, poverty, insecurity, loss of members through permanent separation from those who went to Pennsylvania, numerous deaths from the dreaded tuberculosis, conflicts and misunderstandings with bishops, even the deposition of the general superior and the appointment of a 32 year old Belgian priest (Rev. Edward Joos) — only two years in America — as director and superior. There were also problems of increasing membership in the congregation and schools, a need for expansion, additional buildings.

The young Father Gillet who left his small unprotected community, must have bequeathed something that became the rich soil for God's blessing, as did our pioneer Sisters who displayed an unwavering faith and trust in Divine Providence. (Had they not first been called Sisters of Providence?) They imitated Mary, the perfect servant of the Lord, by finding and responding to the will of God in the circumstances of daily life. (Had they not been called Servants of

Mary?). They committed themselves faithfully to the service of God by exact observance of the Rule (Had not Father Gillet entrusted Mother Theresa with an adaptation of the Redemptorist Rule?).

Despite difficulties, fidelity to this three-fold legacy continued to draw God's special blessing upon the work, and the congregation grew from three Sisters in 1845 to 350 (250 of them living) in 1900, from 44 pupils to 7,000; and from one congregation to three: Monroe (1845), Scranton (1871), and Philadelphia (1872). It was to the Philadelphia congregation that Mother Theresa Maxis returned after spending sixteen years of exile with the Grey Nuns of Ottawa. Until her death in 1892 she was finally "home" with her beloved Immaculate Heart of Mary Sisters.

In 1901 after 43 years as director and superior, Monsignor Joos died. Unrest developed among the Sisters and concern among the clergy about his successor. A wise and understanding Bishop Foley of Detroit decided that "the congregation was now perfectly capable of governing itself." Mother Mechtildis, who had been in office for only seven months, was the first general superior with full power of office. Before the Sisters left Monroe for their mission assignments that year, she gathered them together and assured them that "the congregation is the work of God and not man. He will see it through. We are very grateful to Father, but no one is so essential that his death could destroy a work of God... One fundamental requirement for us is to remain fervent, strong, and faithful to the observance of our Rule." Mother and her assistant, Sister Domitilla, then set to work on the necessary revision of the Rule according to the norms of 1901 — with the hope of receiving final approval from Rome.

1920. The year I entered the convent. The Diamond Jubilee Year of the congregation. The year Rome gave its final approval to the Constitutions. How well I recall that day of excitement in July when the news arrived. How well I also remember that day two-and-a-half years later when I received my own copy of that precious little black book and read with reverence: "The primary end of the congregation is the sanctification of each member by seclusion from the world and the practice of religious observances; the secondary end is the education of youth by all means conformable with the Constitutions." The Rule was indeed a precious document. We read it every Friday during supper, every monthly retreat day, every Ember Day, every day during the annual retreat. We had it practically memorized. Over and over we heard: "Keep the Rule and it will keep you."

Since IHM life for so many years had centered around "Father," it is not surprising that with the approval of the Constitutions it would center around the Mother General. She was the head of the congregation. "It was her duty to watch over exact observance; it was her obligation to see that the requirements of charity were fulfilled, to correct all failures, to visit the houses each year, to confer with the local superiors who reported monthly." Her council of four members was her advisory board.

The sweep of time brought good years. No signs of change appeared. Our prayer life and our school life had priority. Our academic life came next. Our social life was restricted but most of us found it wholesome, enriching, full of memories we still cherish.

To return to the general superiors who were in office during those years. What did they think the future of the congregation would be when they took office? Impenetrable mystery it may be; yet the richness of our inheritance today gives ample proof that they followed the example of Father Gillet, relying on Divine Providence to direct them, to enable them to take risks; seeing and responding to God's will made visible by the needs of the time; being faithful to their commitment as expressed in the Rule, preserving the spirit of Theresa Maxis.

"Dwelling now in light yet ever near." To bring each of these leaders into our presence today, I have selected a quotation from one of their letters regarding the observance of the Rule.

Mother Domitilla: "I am convinced that fidelity to the

Rule must, in a sense, force God to defend us."

Mother Ruth: "Perfect observance is the road to personal holiness required by each member as set forth in the constitutions."

Mother Teresa: "Remember to grow daily in charity and in the exact observance of the Rule." Another Teresa remark: "All action possible, then prayerfully await God" — so different from Mother Theresa Maxis, who once said regretfully, "I tried to force Providence."

Circumstances forced each general superior to go into the "construction business." None was prepared to erect buildings. All realized that "unless the Lord build, they labor in vain." From beginning to end they did trust in Providence, implored the help of Mary to obtain spiritual and temporal aid; asked God to bless each enterprise for his honor and glory and for the advancement of Catholic education.

Each administration had its own distinguishing features during the three-decade span of years: from the approval of the Constitutions to the building of Marygrove College in Detroit; from the fiery holocaust of our beloved St. Mary Academy in Monroe to the long lean years of the Great Depression; from the building of the new motherhouse and academy, the grandeur of its forty-acre frontage to sending forth our first four missionaries to Puerto Rico in 1948. Since that memorable day in August, our eyes have continued to scan the fertile fields of mission lands. To Brazil, Grenada, Honduras, Uganda, Kenya, Ghana, Zimbabwe and South Africa our Sisters have journeyed, learned the language, adapted to the culture, gladly given away their lives in years of service.

And so we come to 1954 and the General Chapter of Elections. In those days preparations were limited. The Rule still said, "It is strictly forbidden to make elections the topic of conversation." How well I remember the day. In the motherhouse chapel before our Lady's altar the capitulars sat in state in the presence of the official designate, Bishop Donnelly of Detroit. The last ballot was counted. The bishop announced my election. Lovingly embracing me,

Mother Teresa said, "I let my mantle fall on you." Whatever divine protection Mother had experienced, she had now passed on to me to sustain me for the next twelve years.

So, to answer the question: What did you think the future of the congregation would be when you took office? Simply that the same Divine Providence that had guided and blessed the IHM Sisters all through the years would continue for years to come. As I look back over the years, I am overwhelmed by what the Lord has done. Buildings. These we can point to with pride, enumerate. They are great to behold; but they are tangibles. What of the intangibles? How can we measure them? The mystery, the gift of each Sister's life? All our ministries, all our caring? The depths of our relationships which "echo from soul to soul and grow forever and ever?"

Inter-congregational meetings were just beginning when I took office. One of the first was in 1956, the organizational meeting of the Conference of Major Superiors (CMSW) which developed later into the Leadership Conference of Women Religious (LCWR). I went truly scared to be among such distinguished people. I remember being wrapped in my long black cloak, looking around and to my surprise discovering that others felt the same way. The meeting gave promise of being a great help to all needing support and courage and developed a strong spirit of unity among women religious in the work of the church. At a subsequent meeting the leaders of the three IHM congregations came together. From that reunion came into being the Tri-IHM Community Conference, one of the authors, our own Sister Thomas Aquinas.

One enactment of the Chapter of 1954 was to begin revision of the Constitutions. Changes of all kinds, even that long ago, were creating problems that involved our ministries. Even in community the stability of our lifestyle was in question. We consulted canonists, other religious congregations. Time passed. We made little progress. Then came 1959. Pope John XXIII declared a Council — Vatican II. All our lives were changed.

As for the second question: How do you see the future of the congregation now? We have changed from commitment to exact observance and strict conformity to just as strong a commitment to accountability and responsible freedom in our personal lives and in our service to the church and world. Changes will continue as time passes, but I believe a true IHM will always have faith and trust in the Providence of God, be attentive to God's will in the needs of the times, and be constantly faithful to her commitment to God as expressed in the Constitutions: "leaving the work to God to bless and make it prosper if it is pleasing to him and useful for the salvation of souls." (Father Louis Florent Gillet, CSSR)

"Waiting In A Traveler's Heart"
Margaret Brennan, IHM
1966-1976

In Lillian Helman's book *Pentimento*, which took the film title *Julia*, the opening lines spoken by Jane Fonda, speak somewhat to the experience I had when drawing together this reflection. In speaking of Julia, Lillian (Jane Fonda) muses...

> "Old paint on canvas, as it ages, sometimes becomes transparent. When that happens it is possible in some pictures, to see the original lines: a tree will show through a woman's dress, a child makes way for a dog, a large boat is no longer on an open sea. What is called pentimento because the painter "repented," changed his mind. Perhaps it would be as well to say that the old conception, replaced by a later choice, is a way of seeing and then seeing again... The paint has aged now and I wanted to see what was there for me once, what is there for me now."

And so, for me, in preparing this reflection, as I recall a view of religious life etched twenty years ago, I see that time and memory have changed the original somewhat. The faint lines and muted colors of *what was there for me once* shows through the brighter landscape of *what is there for me now.* Like Lillian's remembrance of Julia, the person is the same, but she remembers her differently — through the prism of time and memory. In a way she has a different look — not because Julia has changed essentially — but because Lillian has.

When I look back over the years 1966-1976, exact dates and times, persons and places, have often faded away. What remain are experiences, feelings and memories — seen differently now through the prism of time and memory.

The heady reality of Vatican II that broke out into our lives in 1966, and forever changed our understanding of religious life, had begun to push its way into my consciousness, somewhat like little plants that grow through cracks in a pavement, during the six previous years. Two kinds of experiences in the community inaugurated this significant beginning. One was the experience of working on our first revised constitutions. The other was working with the novices.

Of the hundreds of hours spent on that initial revision, one meeting in particular remains etched in my mind. Reflecting on the experience of the Council bishops as they sought to understand the nature of the church and its role in the modern world, the committee came to a sobering conclusion that the structure and articulation of our lives as religious, spelled out in constitutions which had formed and guided IHMs for generations, could not be "patched up," changed here and there. We had to acknowledge that it no longer expressed adequately who we were and who we were called to be in a church which no longer separated itself from the world, a church which acknowledged the universal call to holiness, and recognized the vocation of all the baptized to further its mission.

The other experience was that of living and working with the novices — the generation of the 60s. Their insistent and insightful questioning drove little wedges of truth into my mind that I could no longer ignore. Nor could looking over my glasses and wagging my finger with the admonition,

"Little Sister, you came to join a community — not to found one," assuage the growing awareness that a new reality was breaking in on us — insistently and irrevocably.

Nevertheless, in spite of these encroaching signs, apostolic religious life for women on the eve of the Council was still, basically, a hierarchically structured, semi-monastic form of life. The 1917 Code of Canon Law had prescribed numerous regulations regarding religious governance, the profession and practice of the vows, the formation of novices, the exercise of the apostolate. These were reflected in rules of life that governed every moment of the day. Elements of cloister and separation from the world curtailed contact with "seculars," which was limited to the hours dedicated to the exercise of the apostolate and occasional home visits. The works of religious were basically institutional and carried out in most cases under the mandate of the local bishop. The original apostolic impetus and charisms, which gave birth to the congregation were, as a result, often submerged and lost under prescriptions which hindered rather than enhanced the purposes for which we were founded though we did not recognize it then.

As the congregation prepared for a general chapter just as the Council ended, the new winds of change were already blowing about, and the revised constitutions had attempted to articulate what this might mean for the expression of our lives.

The chapter delegates of 1966 dealt with soul-sized issues in a spirit of joy and enthusiasm. The Council documents became a kind of "vade mecum" in our deliberations and our renewal built on their gospel principles, avoiding admonitions and anathemas. I think we believed that our adaptation to the post-Vatican II world would move ahead smoothly and serenely with a measured pace — even though one of the delegates prophetically warned us that "if we changed our pocket-laps, the whole habit would go."

Although the chapter took bold stands and initiated brave new directions, it left most of the implementation to what was called "General Government" — meaning the

General Superior and the Council. This was in keeping with the accepted traditional form of religious governance that has been operative in the church. But a new spirit had been unleashed whose force was not initially reckoned with. In the early months of the renewal a growing sense of personal initiative and responsibility expressed itself in what touched us most closely and immediately — our own persons.

My recollections of what seemed to be interminable Council meetings those early months and years, were filled with what I now call the "trauma of the trivia" as we began to live without the structures and the strictures of the past. Local superiors (yes! we still had them then) came to monthly meetings fairly bristling with questions that demanded answers — and indicated that things were getting out of hand. More directives were needed.

> . . . if the modified habit concept called for a round collar, what shall we say about those who are beginning to wear pointed collars?

> . . . were we conscious that some sisters were wearing blue blouses?

> . . . that some sisters were departing from the modified concept and designing suits of their own?

> . . . that sisters were seen on the Marygrove campus eating Dairy Queens?

At one council meeting I recall waiting anxiously as Sister Robertine phoned a Detroit convent, hopefully to dispel the report that the local superior had come to breakfast on a Saturday morning with curlers in her hair! (Alas! the rumor was true.)

We laugh now that such "trivia" troubled and even traumatized some of us — but it was a necessary and inevitable part of the passage to the real and deeper meaning and consequences of what the adaptation of religious life really called us to.

In 1967, two years after the close of the Council, Edward Schillebeeckx wrote the following with an unsuspected sense of prophecy:

> "The 'adaptation of the religious life' must be, first and foremost, a re-evangelizing of all its structures. The consequences of this conciliar maxim are more numerous than a superficial reading of it would seem to indicate. The text gives the Church an inspiration whose charismatic consequences, I feel, cannot even be surmised at this moment. But eventually this 'supreme rule' will break through, without any clashes, we trust, though some will occur."
>
> Edward Schillebeeckx, *Vatican II: The Real Achievement,* p. 46.

The charismatic consequences of the re-evangelizing of religious life did break through and the clashes occurred as well

By 1969 when the congregation prepared for the special renewal chapter prescribed by Pope Paul VI in his letter *Ecclesiae Sanctae,* we had more deeply internalized the meaning and implications of the Vatican documents on religious life, and had begun to interpret their pastoral meaning in the ambience of other documents — notably *The Church in the Modern World, The Decree on Missionary Activity,* and *The Declaration on Religious Freedom.*

This chapter marked a significant difference in our self-understanding and it became clearer that our concept of religious life was irretrievably marked with new and fundamental directions evidenced in:

> ...a shift of accent in prayer which did not denigrate its contemplative stance, but sought rather to discover God in the human experiences of life.

> ...the search for the articulation of an apostolic spirituality that recognized human experience as a locus of God's on-going revelation.

. . . a shift from separation from the world to involvement in it.

. . . a move from religious life seen essentially as a personal consecration to include prophecy, witness/diakonia.

. . . a less passive assent to obedience and monarchical, hierarchical structures.

. . . a move away from monastic forms of religious life and sacral symbols (religious habits, titles, and names)

. . . a feel for history, evolution, and non-static world views which relativized the note of permanency inherent in the traditional concept of the vows.

. . . an emphasis on notions of mutuality, participation, collegiality, subsidiarity, the servant role of authority.

. . . a conviction that constitutions were to be primarily inspirational and visionary rather than prescriptive and cautionary.

. . . a belief that law was to provide for the rights of the individual.

In general, the liberal view of Vatican II tended to move from a focus on the sacral, corporate stance of religious institutes in the church to one whose focus was mission, together with an accent on personal dignity, responsibility, the journey to human fulfillment, especially through the interpersonal lives of the unique individuals called to celibate commitment in community.

Yet, in spite of all the positive movements forward, the years of the late sixties and early seventies were ones of turmoil for both religious congregations and for the hierarchy as well. A mixture of both negative and positive elements impinged on the experience of the renewal of religious life. There was both challenge and confusion in internalizing the new concepts initiated by the Council.

Congregationally, we struggled with new forms of government — provincial boundaries and membership — and living "as if." The passage of "Proposal C" in Michigan brought about the closing of many parochial schools. The movement into new ministries was accompanied by struggles with discernment with what was a church ministry and what was not. Perhaps most painful, was the departure of so many of our sisters and friends into other ways of life. How we dreaded those long lists at the end of each year! For me personally, speaking with 200 sisters who struggled with their own personal calling brought the realization that God's will was not a "blue print" drawn-up from all eternity, but a dynamic living force, whose meaning we must continually search for in the depths of our heart. Watching the novitiate shrink from sixty, seventy or eighty to twenty, fifteen or ten brought a numbing fear, as we looked toward our future.

The diverse views of renewal, based on differing ecclesiologies in the documents of Vatican II, brought pain and internal division between individuals within communities and between communities themselves. This was concretized in the tension among major superiors. In opposition to the more liberal views of the *LCWR*, Leadership Conference of Women Religious, a significant number of general superiors formed a conference of their own under the title *Consortium Perfectae Caritatis.* Many Bishops found themselves divided in their allegiance to one group or another, and in time the *Sacred Congregation For Religious and Secular Institutes* entered into the controversy in an attempt to bring a unity, which was never successfully resolved.

On the positive side, the call to be in the world and to serve the poor and marginated, led many into ministries among the elderly, prisoners, migrants, the black community, native peoples. We began to see that ways of fulfilling our educational mission had been broadly expanded, and that it was, in fact, inseparable from our call to work for justice. Large and spacious convents were often relinquished to live religious life among the people we served. Religious habits and enclosed monastic lives with structured prayer forms gave way to secular dress and new forms of prayer and community life developed to energize the faith-sharing and life of religious. Heightened social consciousness motivated many to challenge unjust political and economic structures at home and abroad.

For many bishops, the move of women religious into diverse ministries of a non-institutional character, loosened the ties between the religious and the hierarchy in the ordering of apostolic works. The removal of religious habits and a non-structured way of life brought tension and misunderstanding, which in some cases reached crisis proportions, as in the case of the California Immaculate Heart of Mary Sisters and the Glenmary Community, who were pressured into non-canonical status.

From Rome, the *Sacred Congregation For Religious and Secular Institutes* reacted with alarm and concern; and not without great difficulties did North American religious congregations attempt to reflect their experience and have it understood. In some instances apostolic visitations were conducted, prompted by the pleas of more traditionally oriented groups of sisters from within their own communities. This sometimes resulted in divisions which hardened into irrevocable splits.

In this regard, I want to say that in spite of the very real struggles in our own congregation — in spite of the differences of opinion and the very real concern of many — our loyalty to ourselves, to our past, and to our future as a congregation, kept us from writing or appealing to Rome to settle our differences — and all of us know that we had very powerful, dynamic, and committed members who could easily have led us in splinter groups.

Our experience of religious life in the late sixties and early seventies was, moreover, carried out in a context within our own country that was marked by struggle and turmoil — all of which shaped our social consciousness and sharpened our understanding of ministry: Selma and the Civil Rights

Movement, the Vietnam War and the ministry for Peace, the assassination of Martin Luther King and Robert Kennedy, Watergate and a growing sense of political responsibility and advocacy, the women's movement and the growing lines of a feminist theology.

Looking back now at 1976 when I left office, I can only say that I believe the direction that the renewal took far exceeded our early conception of it. The "experiments" in our life became a "way of life" and "change" was the constant we dealt with.

It was readily seen that the final form the changes would take were not yet clear — nor would they be for some time to come.

In short, a paradigm shift was taking place, and what it meant was yet to be seen.

One of the sisters with whom I live (Jean Bartunek, RSCJ) is an organizational psychologist who teaches at Boston College. She has just published an article in *Administrative Science Quarterly* entitled "Changing Interpretive Schemes and Organizational Restructuring: The Example of a Religious Order." It is from her that I gained a final insight as I reflect back from now to what I saw then.

Making use of the research of organizational theory, she successfully argues that although "environmental forces are likely to initiate change in any organization, the way the environment is interpreted by organizational members, affects the type of change that takes place" — and further — "the way the organization's leadership initiates or responds to alternative schemes (that is, ways of understanding ourselves) limits the type of change in understanding that can occur." In other words, the way the congregation's leadership initiates or responds to new ways and understandings, limits or enhances the degree to which the congregation's self-understanding can evolve.

In the light of this insight, I want to say — simply — that as I left a position of leadership, I believe that the congregation had internalized the environmental forces (both from the Vatican Council and our own lived reality) — and that we were beginning to, but had not finished developing a self-understanding as a congregation that expressed who we were in response to these changes. Our norms and world view were in the process of changing dramatically, and a fundamental shift in our sense of mission was following, as an inevitable consequence.

It is a contention of J. Bartunek that change in interpretive schemes "occurs through a dialectical process, in which old and new ways of understanding interact, resulting in a new synthesis."

I believe that this was true for us. Our old and new understanding of our lives and our mission had interacted and was being born of conflict; the uncertainty, the chaos, and the pain — coupled with the conviction and certainty as well, that such interaction would, in time, bring new life.

To discover and find the ways of articulating that new synthesis in structures, that would engage participation of the whole membership without blunting prophetic imagination, was a challenge that remained...these structures would not only be those of our own making, but those enjoined by the church as well.

Conclusion

I have entitled this reflection "Waiting in a Traveler's Heart." The words are taken from Leonard Cohn's *Book of Mercy* — a little volume of thoughts on the mercy of God, whose name and presence "unifies our hearts when they are in a rage of directions, and gently lifts the world into place."

The last line in the book is a beatitude: "Blessed is the one who waits in the traveler's heart for her turning."

Our life and mission is, as that of Jesus, forwarded in a journey. Luke notes how "through towns and villages he went teaching, making his way to Jerusalem" (Lk. 13:22). A temptation for any traveler — and pilgrim — is to "settle down" and to "settle in" — to domesticate the urges and impulses that beckon forward. All persons and groups, and especially institutions, are subject to this subtle temptation in the name of stability and order.

Our turning — our readiness to risk the future can occur, it seems to me, only if we have traveler's hearts — where the waiting is a respite, not a rooting. It is to have a watchful eye on the changing horizon and to know the moment when it is time to have the courage to say, in the words of Walt Whitman:

> "We have stood here like trees in the ground long enough. Let us sail for the open waters where we will have passage."

A Memorable Hour In Religious Life
Mary Kinney, I.H.M.

1976-82

In order to place my reflections in a context, I would like to review some history. In the fall of 1974 a committee was appointed to set in motion processes to study the strengths and weaknesses of our government structures and to involve the IHM Congregation in the formation of a plan that would facilitate our being a Congregation in mission. From the fall of 1974 until the spring of 1976 we as a Congregation were engaged in that process.

As we listened we heard the membership saying; We have been in renewal for a decade. We have gone through a great deal to renew ourselves personally and to come to an understanding of our role as apostolic women in the world. Our individual lifestyles and our community living have changed a great deal in the past decade. We need to address some other areas of our lives.

The congregation brought to the fore other areas: We needed to feel good about ourselves as a group — our corporate image had been blurred. We sensed that in some way our public image had been linked to what we did in ministry. We had a reputation for being excellent educators. The loss of schools and institutions called us to do some re-thinking in the area of ministry. We needed healing. Changes during renewal had alienated some groups both within and outside of the congregation. We had been in provinces for a number of years, and questions of autonomy and decisions that impacted the life of the total congregation needed to be addressed. There was a need to develop structures that would ensure our acting interdependently in the congregation. There was also a need to collaborate with other congregations in addressing compensation issues for women religious in Michigan and throughout the United States. We needed to work not only with a formation program but to develop a life-long planning process which would enable our women to be prepared for ministry. We heard the membership calling us to face the realities of our lives and to do some long-range planning in regard to our decreasing membership; the use and ownership of our institutions; a development program that would ease the burden placed on our earners; setting some priorities for ministries; planning ahead for the care of our own infirm and aging members.

Having spent time listening to the congregation, we worked through a goal-setting process. By 1977 we had established goals for ourselves. The goals were a reflection of the needs raised up by the congregation together with our vision.

In our first goal we envisioned the congregation to be, and to be recognized as a congregation for mission with its lifestyle and community living being consonant with a life that is joyful, loving, giving, simple. We envisioned the members of the congregation choosing lifestyles both personal and institutional in the spirit of global solidarity, futuristic consciousness and Christ-centered austerity.

In our second goal we envisioned each sister being able to deepen the consciousness of her personal gifts, relationship with Jesus, and understanding of being an apostolic woman religious; her sense that belonging to a congregation includes giving and sharing personal gifts and responsibilities, as well as calling forth the gifts of others; and that the interchange is essential for her own full development and that of the corporate body.

In our third goal we envisioned the congregation becoming more fully conscious of who we are as women religious in today's world; where we have come from: by an ongoing reflection on our history and the charism that energized us; where we are going: by deliberate futurizing and long-range planning in all areas and by modeling and encouraging collaborative models.

In our fourth goal we envisioned the congregation discussing and articulating a congregational thrust in ministry that would be: broad in scope and deeply rooted in union with Jesus; directed to the abandoned, to healing and enabling humankind, to the aging, to those groups with whom the development of lay leadership would require more input because of their needs, to ministries which would be directed toward systemic transformation by using the tools of social analysis and theological reflection.

In our fifth goal we envisioned ourselves managing our material resources in order to: free sisters for ministry and from financial anxiety; direct our resources to the service of our ministries, and the transformation of the socio-economic order; work to eliminate the injustices which contributed to our financial situation, namely exploitation of women in church structures.

We envisioned ourselves doing this: by being responsible and accountable at the Central level, by collaborative planning with Provincial Adminstrations, by involving the membership in fostering the sense of interdependence in the use of our resources (cf. Chapter Report of Central Administration, 1976-1982).

In nourishing and deepening values and beliefs with regard to building relationships, collaborative actions, team efforts and interdependent modes of operating, we hoped to enable our members not only to grow individually, but to grow together as a community.

To realize our visionary goals, we entered into decision-making processes that frequently involved the total congregation, such as the decisions regarding our schools, as well as reflection, study and discussion on our Constitutions. Involving the congregation in these processes enabled us to set directions, and own decisions, that would impact our preferred future. I believe too, the times of coming together to think, study, plan, pray, celebrate enabled us to come to a sense of corporateness which seemed to be needed.

During the first years after Vatican II, within the congregation, persons and growth of persons were given great emphasis — and rightly so — for all the reasons we know so well; however, sometimes, I believe we emphasized that in a way that fostered the growth of persons as individuals but not as individuals in community. The values of collaboration, interdependence, corporateness are not values of our American society. We live in a world that reflects a basic economic philosophy which says if each person pursues her own self-interest the whole will benefit, and thus the question becomes: How can we organize ourselves in such a way that each one can prevent others from interfering with one's self-interest? The question should be: How do we live and work together to accomplish our reason for being together, that is to bring about the mission of Jesus?

Our basic challenge is the never-ending process of individual growth beyond the stage of individual autonomy. I believe the trend toward individual autonomy has impacted our lifestyles and community living. As Christians we are called to be communities, where members of the group love and trust each other enough to share where they have or have not encountered God, communities where the members receive sufficient affirmation from each other to be comfortable while being open and trusting with others, exposing their weaknesses, their poverty, and accepting those of others. We all know there are days when we must be literally carried to hope, and to God, as in the gospel story of the paralytic who was brought by his friends to Jesus to be healed. Jesus accepted and healed the paralytic in response to the love and trust of his friends. (cf. Contemporary Meditations on Hope, John Heagle, p. 73-74).

Sometimes we need to be carried by the trust and encouragement of our sisters in community. We also need the love and esteem of one another. Dick Westley in his book *Morality and Its Beyond* in speaking of self-esteem and self-worth says:

> *. . . Self-esteem is an absolutely essential ingredient of a truly human life.* . .self-esteem, contrary to what the world might lead us to believe, is not something I can simply do for or by myself. It is precisely because my self-esteem is tied up with and depends on others that I have no simple and direct way of getting it. . .

> . . . therefore, we must somehow incarnate it (self-esteem) in visible signs and symbols. Those signs and symbols must also be recognized by others, who *then* must show us that they recognized our personal worth. . .

> (*Morality and Its Beyond*, Dick Westley, p. 18-19)

I believe we are beginning to own the pluralism that is among us and to experience it as enriching ourselves and for the people to whom we minister. Recently, the Christian Theological Seminary in Indianapolis hosted a day of reflection with Raymond Brown, who was sharing some thoughts from his book, *The Churches the Apostles Left Behind.*

Fr. Brown used three accounts of the Passion to show the diverse emphasis we find in the gospel accounts. In Mark's version after the supper, there is a very negative approach. We read Jesus was condemned, abandoned, betrayed. The apostles fled.

Luke reflects a positive, healing approach with Jesus being more concerned for others than for himself. In John's account we see Jesus being sustained and supported by the Father, in full control. The Passion is over when Jesus, in control, says: "It is consummated." (Talk given by Fr. Raymond Brown on his book, *The Churches the Apostles Left Behind.*)

From these reflections Fr. Brown pointed out that from the very beginning of the church there was diversity of interpretation of experiences with Jesus. Diversity can be used profitably and to enrich us. The church is reluctant to take one view.

I believe we are still working at the integration of community and ministry — not identifying ministry as each individual having a job and community merely as the place one lives while one has that job. I hope we keep before us the image of a community of disciples, who are united in their call to serve, and who share their faith experiences in such a way that their community life impacts their ministry, and their ministry impacts their living together.

I see us still struggling with questions regarding leadership, authority, obedience and accountability. I believe, as was pointed out to us by the committee working on the Constitutions, that these are areas we need to spend some time on and articulate what meanings they have for us. We need to ask what understandings of these concepts we wish to pass on to the next generation of IHM sisters.

In a more practical vein, I believe we need to ask ourselves from time to time, if there is anything we do or don't do, after we call women forth to serve in leadership roles in the Congregation, that hampers them or holds them back from using their best gifts. I do not believe there is a contradiction between authority and servanthood. Some secular models include a good public servant who carries out the will of people and acts as a facilitator of a group, a catalyst of group action who simply stays in a non-directive role.

Christian leadership may do all these things at one time or another, but I believe, we as members, need to encourage our leaders to speak clearly and prophetically the hard sayings of Jesus to us. We need to encourage them to lead. "*Journey Into Weakness: An Exploration of Servant Leadership*," Gene Beerense — Reprint from *Sojourners*, February, 1980).

I see us making an effort to transcend our own individual limitations, and pass over to a new consciousness of the larger community of which we are a part, the global community and its needs. I believe we are blessed to have a group of women, who make up our Vice-Province, who though small in number, are fully alive and committed to responding to global needs. They keep these needs before us even as I see them struggling to live, work, pray together. To me this says our missionary spirit is alive and well.

I see us struggling with the injustice and oppression of women in the world and the church today — working through the process of liberation, not only for ourselves but for all women and their need for just salaries, pensions, social security and acceptance into decision-making roles.

In all our ministries, I see us working for peace and justice in our world, and paying the price for that stance by being advocates for the poor and oppressed. I see us choosing ministries that fit our gifts and not being defensive about where we are serving, knowing that we are all working for the same purposes.

With the church, I feel we are in gentle but consistent dialogue not only for approval of our Constitutions but also on issues touching women in ministry. We need to be as honest and open in working with the church as we were in working through renewal in the congregation. Working for internal justice is usually more painful and costly. In all the struggles we enter into to make this world a better place for all peoples, I know we are mindful that the weaknesses we find in the church, society and the congregation are already present potentially within ourselves, and we know God works through our weaknesses.

Our congregation began without wealth, land or possession, but we didn't begin without love for and belief in one another, and a belief in our call to discipleship and ministry to God's people. From the earliest days and down to our own time, our lives have been marked by a deep commitment to prayer, the Eucharist, justice, peace and ministries that responded to the needs of the times. Reflection on our history engenders hope, because whatever challenge or crisis we faced, we did so with deep faith and courage.

When the history of our years is written, let us hope it can be said of us:

> "In spite of everything they absorbed all the promise of the Vatican Council and all its shock. They lived a memorable hour in the Church's history for they began a new Pentecost without a Reformation, a Revolution without a schism, an aggiornamento without a refusal of the past. They were willing to stand fast in the darkness. And they lighted the world with their love and fidelity . . . "

(cf. Homily by Anthony Padovano)

Focus For The Future

Carol Quigley, I.H.M.

(1982-   )

My vision of the future of religious life has deepened rather than changed since 1982 because experience has confirmed the truth of what I saw less clearly then, and because I have not been disappointed in the hopes I have held for several years. My reflections, then, will touch on some events of these two years which give the present context for religious life of the future, and then share my vision of the future which I believe to be our communal vision.

These two and one-half years, of course, have brought unexpected joys and sorrows. I could not foresee many events: the invasion of Grenada by the U.S.; the tragic murder of a member of our own congregation; the publication of *Essential Elements*; increased involvement by Rome in the internal matters of U.S. congregations; some church understandings of authority in tension with theology; the growing gap between the pristine values of our nation and current national and international relations; or the rising tide of fundamentalist religion and political conservatism. Nor could I anticipate these movements: the congregation's public positions on the side of the poor, e.g., Central America, Puerto Rico, gun control; the growth of pride in our members in their being IHM; the deep desire for interprovincial communication; the degree of intercongregational support in light of common challenges (LCWR 8/84); our deeper commitment to peacemaking through our ministries; the maturing of the feminist movement; the Bishops' Pastorals: *The Challenge of Peace: God's Promise and Our Response*, 1983; *Pastoral Letter on Catholic Social Teaching and the U.S. Economy* (First Draft, 1984); and the future one on women; and the increased understanding of networking.

These events have not blurred my vision, but have, rather, focused it more clearly. Because we are a pontifical congregation founded in the United States, the larger ecclesial societal realities play upon our religious life. Because we believe we are primarily a people of God, who belong to a Catholic church and who, for the most part, are citizens of the United States, we create our future in a context. How we see the church colors, perhaps even clarifies our vision for the future of religious life. Where we stand influences what we see; to whom we listen influences what we hear; what we do influences who we are.

What is my analysis of our church and world? In the past few months I have heard two speakers refer to the 1960's as difficult times. These speakers were not reactionary; perhaps they were more realistic than I. Surely there were difficulties in every sphere of our lives during the 60's. Yet, from my perspective, the decade of the 60's was exciting, dynamic, challenging. It was a moment of radical re-vision of the U.S. as a nation and of the church as universal. The idealism that soared then is still carrying us forward. The era of the "three Johns" — John XXIII, John Kennedy, and Cardinal John Dearden — was alive and life-giving.

The vision that emerged in the 60's came under question in the subsequent decades. Today we witness what I consider a very different set of challenges. In our United States we are faced with choices that will not only shape our future but determine if we have a future. The values crisis of our nation makes a mockery of the fundamental beliefs of our ancestors. Most of us here are the beneficiaries of their immigration to this country.

Today some social scientists would have us believe that the poor are to blame for their poverty. And yet, last year 15 million of the world's children died of malnutrition. Such victims cannot be held responsible for their own poverty. In our own country, witness the growth of the lower class through reduced government spending and unemployment, especially among the elderly and women. If we, as a country, do not feed the hungry that we see, how can we be moved to do justice to those we do not see?

How can we be touched by a nuclear winter when we do not believe the warning that "even a limited nuclear war will generate enough soot and dust to shield a substantial portion of the earth from sunlight, perhaps for months, potentially causing the extinction of numerous plants and animals, including humans." (*Science*, July 6, 1984) The user nation would be as vulnerable as all others.

Violence in a multiplicity of forms has become all too common — personally, nationally, internationally or should we say multi-nationally. Quality of education in our public schools has declined greatly in the past decade, making Catholic schools a safe (even literally) alternative. The ignorance of the masses feeds on a growing illiteracy even among high school graduates. Economically we experience what Michael Harrington has labeled "socialism for the rich and free enterprise for the poor."

Given the challenges which face society, the church as leaven for society is no less challenged. As bearer of the joys and sorrows of the world as well as in its own life as an institution, the church must constantly re-examine itself. In the past year, we have observed a steady trend to return to the pre-conciliar modes of thinking, acting, governing. We observe also an increase of expressions which would dichotomize elements we have since Vatican II attempted to integrate: faith and justice, reflection and action, sacred and secular, church and world, men and women. We know of women religious who, because they took the Council so seriously, have now come under questioning in at least seventeen instances. We learn of the threat to academic freedom of theologians by those in authority. What has happened to the adage we learned in our theology classes even before the Council, "When the masters disagree, the students are free?" Theodore Ross, S.J., faculty member at Catholic Theological Union, reminds us that the role of the priest, prophet, and king, taken respectively by the faithful, the theologians, and church leaders must be kept in creative tension if the church is to be the church of Jesus Christ.

The Church and Society are two lenses leading to a single vision — one serving to focus the other. The relationship we see between the two affects our vision. In the early 1950's Richard Niebuhr wrote a timeless treatise called *Christ and Culture* in which he suggests that the view of that relationship is pivotal to the service of church ministers. I summarize it: One model is Christ against culture in which the church and the world by way of application are put at odds with each other in competition, even contempt; the second model would be that of Christ within culture in which the two are synthesized beyond clear distinction. In the 1984 political campaigns we saw a blurring of those lines both on the part of church people and politicians alike. The third model would be that of Christ transforming culture, particularly in the image of the church as people of God.

More recently Paul VI reminded us in his exhortation *Evangelii Nuntiandi:* "Though independent of cultures, the Gospel and evangelization are not necessarily incompatible with them; rather they are capable of permeating them all without becoming subject to any one of them." Not only do I subscribe to this last model, I would add that as Christ transforms culture, each culture in turn offers some gospel gift that enriches the Church and strengthens its universality.

The new Church of Vatican II has had a generation of gestation. It is coming to birth and the pain is mounting in frequency and intensity. If the Church is midwife of a new world, are we women religious midwives of that new Church? Increasingly we hear from priests and bishops that we have led the renewal. They correctly cite our education as the reason we took the lead. As far back as 1953 our IHM Sisters led in the Sister Formation Movement. Today I ask: What do the IHM Sisters of 1984 offer to the future?

At this point in history, I envision a new flowering of our charism: peacemaking based on hope moving toward unity. During the leadership of these past three superiors general, we have changed the articulation of our charism from "self-abnegation and renouncement of self will" to: "The love of Jesus Christ unites us in community and impels us to proclaim the good news of salvation." What has not changed is the identification with the mission of Jesus, which is to return the world to God, to redeem. Inherently reconciling, inherently peacemaking, our spirit has never been more needed than in this day and age.

In 1980 at our congregational assembly, we IHM's gave our strongest support to the goal of peacemaking. Deepest in the heart of the congregation is that desire to bring all together in Jesus. It is the greatest need in the world today and pivotal to its very continuance. Peacemaking is not only an urgent issue, it is the core of the gospel and of our history as a congregation. Increased militarization and the tenor of U.S. elected officials signal grave danger. Because of the drain on our resources the poor increase, as Pope Paul VI reminded us, even if the arms are not used, their proliferation is such a drain on material resources that human needs are unmet. In effect, the number of poor persons increases. The nuclear threat, I would add, can kill our spirit even if the arms are not employed because of the havoc with which we live.

We have already taken steps toward a new depth of expressing our charism. In a world torn by violence we continue to offer hope. We are viewed by other religious as a source and resource on these issues. Social justice, I would say, is "in the bloodstream of the congregation." The vast majority of our members engage in some issues in a systemic manner, depending on the needs of the people they serve. We have taken public stands on the side of the poor regarding their human rights as individuals and as nations. Our corporate stance on Central America is timely and urgently needed. Have we re-read it and pondered it anew? Have we asked ourselves how it can be used now locally and congregationally?

A few days ago, on the first anniversary of the murder of Sister John Clement, our IHM victim of violence, I invited the congregation and the college communities to join corporate strengths in supporting a proposal before Mayor Young to control handguns in the city of Detroit — once again nationally notorious for its violence.

In the current issue of *Sojourners*, (Nov. 8, 1984), devoted to the theme of violence against women, Ginny Soley writes; "Certainly one of the factors that helps create a violent society is the acceptance of violence as a way of life. While many of us grow more concerned about violence, the evidence and general acceptance of that violence is increasing within popular mainstream culture." IHM's on the other hand see peacemaking as a way of life.

Our future will grow out of our present as we read the signs of the times in light of our charism and the gospel, and become leaders in reconciling, in peacemaking. Can we preach peacemaking by our very lives, letting our most important values be our priorities, letting go peacefully of whatever binds us, be it righteousness, a rigidity, a richness? Can we be counter-cultural by our very pace of living? Can we model to other women and groups, and learn from them what it is to be womanly, discover together just how much women and peacemaking can partner? Can we be disarming because we gently speak the truth (being well-informed) and express ourselves non-violently?

Ecclesially we are beginning to exercise our peacemaking efforts, especially non-violent resolution of conflict. As we move toward a more adult relationship with the church, our peacemaking will develop and deepen. As the conviction among the people of God grows that we are the people of God, many of our discoveries as a congregation will help us in our ministry, just as what we have learned in ministry influences our life as a congregation.

The role of law in our lives will emerge into more mature expression. Historical perspective, weighing of authority, and cultural nuances will focus our response to the institutional Church. As we direct our own future, we exercise our authority as a congregation to author the IHM vision based on that of Jesus Christ. In our ministry we continue to direct our efforts on the side of the poor through direct service, through advocacy, through education of all ages with emphasis on critical thinking. Will we in our corporate ministries, even as we relinquish ownership of our educational institutions and create new relationships with them, continue to influence the vision of those ministries? In other corporate ministries, — those without walls — can we pledge our service as provinces or as a congregation for, let us say, five to ten years?

Our long-range vision of peacemaking is based on hope. This hope is a confidence in our potential for growth. I envision a greater reconciliation — or integration — of the very elements of our life together. Can we resolve a certain competition between ministry and community, and even prayer? For years, to be a community woman was a greater good than involvement in the apostolate. Now, at times, I feel concerned that zeal in the name of ministry could resemble the frenetic pace, the overextension, the workaholism of the U.S. culture. In our prayer, what were called distractions are now the starting point as we take our experience, reflect upon it, and find God in it. Will these three facets — prayer, ministry and community, distinct yet vital components of our mission — encircle, embrace each other? In our governance within the congregation, I hope we can move toward a more organic model with even greater participation of the membership in the visioning, the direction-setting, the deeper commitment of all to live out all that we decide in community.

I see our future as being yet more prophetic in terms of our resources. We have had the benefit of years of foresight in congregational planning. We have invested our material resources in such a way that our values as a congregation can be expressed at stockholders' meetings, in housing for the poor at lower rates of interest. Our future will heighten the importance of basic communities in which members as peers will discern ministry, evaluate quality of cummunity life, and even be accountable financially. Potentially this movement might well bring to a new reality the partnering of the common and individual good.

As for human resources, if we decrease, let it be experienced as part of the paschal mystery, not with a sense of failure. Let us foster new life not only through the increase of new members but also by sponsoring new forms of committed life.

Finally, within all of our structures, programs, policies, procedures, I hope we can, as feminist Carol Gilligan suggests, move from the logic of justice to an ethics of care, not abandoning a principled understanding of fairness, yet focusing on non-violent conflict resolution, belief in the restorative activity of care.

As you have listened to this list of societal and ecclesial elements in our context today, you could become disheartened. Yet, recalling that our charism expresses Jesus' mission of reconciliation, I would submit that we as a congregation are most relevant in situations at odds with the gospel. Our history and heritage have equipped us to know that confrontation is part of our distinct gift to our society and church.

After more than two years in this ministry I believe that there is a grace of office, yet I believe it is the grace given to every minister in whatever service she performs. I experience that grace in specific moments of great need; I experience it continuously in the awareness that there is no time I would rather serve in leadership and no group I would rather lead in service than you.

Finally, my vision is to enable, to nurture, to energize a new kind of unity in the congregation, not the uniformity of the past, nor simply a summation of the nearly one thousand individual members; rather a synergy in which each individual brings the gift of her own person, places it freely in the treasury of the community where it is enriched by interrelation with others, then given yet more freely to the people of God through whom one meets the Giver of all gifts; a unity which expresses our commitment with each other; a unity which encourages a deep relationship with at least a few persons and openness to many, often coming from very different perspectives, backgrounds; a unity which positively builds up the other, calling her to her own fullness of truth and life; a unity through which a new meaning of corporate, of body, of community is born, a unity which leads us in prayer to the One before whom we are all merely, yet magnificently, creatures, equals, sisters; a unity, finally, which will become ultimate when categories such as congregation, church, and nations will fall into irrelevance before God.

The Contributors

MARGARET R. BRENNAN, IHM

Margaret Brennan, IHM, is an Immaculate Heart of Mary Sister from Monroe, Michigan. She obtained her doctorate in theology from St. Mary's College, Notre Dame. As general superior of her order, president of the Leadership Conference of Women Religious, and councillor to the International Union of Superiors General, she worked extensively with women religious in areas of renewal, ministry, and spirituality. Her insights in this regard have been shared in major addresses to a number of societies and religious congregations and in articles which have been published in periodicals and books. Currently, she is professor of pastoral theology and director of continuing education at Regis College in the Toronto School of Theology. Her areas of particular interest are in feminist theology, ministry, and the relation of spirituality and culture.

JULIANA CASEY, IHM

Juliana Casey, IHM, was provincial of the Northeast province of the Sisters, Servants of the Immaculate Heart of Mary (Monroe, Michigan) 1979-1985. She holds the Doctorate of Sacred Theology from the Catholic University of Louvain,

Belgium. The author of a commentary on "Epistle to the Hebrews"as well as numerous articles, Casey has lectured on peacemaking, women's issues, and scripture throughout the United States and Europe. From 1981-1983, she served as LCWR representative to the U.S. Bishops' Committee for the Pastoral, "The Challenge of Peace: God's Promise and Our Response." She is the author of *WHERE IS GOD NOW? NUCLEAR TERROR, FEMINISM, AND THE SEARCH FOR GOD.* Casey is presently assistant professor of New Testament at Mundelein College, Chicago, Illinois.

EMILY GEORGE, RSM

Formerly Assistant General Adminstrator for the Sisters of Mercy of the Union and Provincial Administrator of the Province of Detroit, Emily George was a visiting scholar at Notre Dame University at the time of her death in 1984. An educator by training, Emily held a doctorate in history from St. Louis University. She taught history at Mercy College of Detroit before being named President of the College in 1967. While on the General Administrative Team, Emily directed the activities of the Church Institute Committee which produced a historical study on the canonical regulation of women's religious communities. Publications include political biographies of Martha W. Griffiths, Zachariah Chandler and William Woodbridge. At the time of her death she was engaged in research on Ellen Gates Starr, co-founder with Jane Addams of Chicago's Hull House.

ANNA MARIE GRIX, IHM

Experienced in the fields of education and administration, Anna Marie Grix, IHM, is presently retired at the IHM Motherhouse in Monroe, Michigan, serving as pastoral minister to the infirm Sisters in St. Mary Health Care Center. During her years of active ministry, Sister Anna

Marie served as principal of several large schools in the Detroit area and spent seven years as Dean of Students at Marygrove College in Detroit, Michigan. After her twelve years as General Superior of the Sisters, Servants of the Immaculate Heart of Mary, she pioneered the IHM mission in Uganda, teaching English to the Bannabikara Sisters in Rwanda. After returning to the United States she served as motherhouse administrator and later as pastoral minister and teacher in the inner city of Detroit.

MARY KINNEY, IHM

Mary Kinney, IHM, holds an M.Ed. in Administration from the University of Detroit. She has had a wide range of experience in congregational leadership during the ongoing developing years of Religious Life both as provincial and general superior; facilitated groups of the Leadership Conference of Women Religious at national and regional levels. Experienced as an administrator in the Detroit Archdiocesan Parochial School System, she is presently an Associate Director of Urban Ministry Study, Archdiocese of Indianapolis, working with 22 inner-city parishes.

ANTHONY R. KOSNIK

A priest of the Archdiocese of Detroit, Anthony R. Kosnik has spent most of his teaching career forming priests and ministers for service in the church. Formerly on the faculty and Dean of Theology at SS. Cyril and Methodius Seminary, he is presently Director of the Program of Pastoral Ministry at Marygrove College, Detroit. He was chairperson for the Catholic Theological Society of America Study on Human Sexuality and is currently a member of the CTSA Board. He has lectured widely and has published in a variety of journals including *The Jurist, Linacre Quarterly, The Catholic Mind* and *Catholic Hospital Progress.*

CAROL QUIGLEY, IHM

Carol Quigley, IHM, is currently serving as president of the Sisters, Servants of the Immaculate Heart of Mary, Monroe, Michigan. She holds a Master's Degree in Theology from the Institute of Christian Thought, University of St. Michael College, Toronto, Ontario. Her prior ministry experience included education, missionary work in Recife, Brazil, and coordination of ministries for the IHM congregation. Active in the Leadership Conference of Women Religious for many years, she was elected its vice-president for 1985-1986 and is serving as president in 1986-1987.

SANDRA MARIE SCHNEIDERS, IHM

Sandra Schneiders, IHM, is an Associate Professor of New Testament Studies and Spirituality, Jesuit School of Theology/Graduate Theological Union, Berkeley, California. She holds an S.T.D. from Pontifical Gregorian University, Rome and an S.R.L. from Institut Catholique, Paris. She is affiliated with several professional organizations including *American Academy of Religion, Catholic Theological Society of America*; is listed in several distinguished directories: *Who's Who of Women, Foremost Women of the Twentieth Century, International Directory of Distinguished Leadership*. Fluent in a number of languages, Schneiders has written extensively in religious journals in this country and in Europe; among the most recent are: "Spiritual Direction," *Horizons* II (Spring 1984), "New Testament Reflections on Peace and Nuclear Arms," *Catholics and Nuclear War: A commentary on "The Challenge of Peace," The U.S. Bishops' Pastoral Letter on War and Peace*, ed. P.J. Murnion. New York: Crossroad, 1983.